PECK'S BAD BOY ABROAD: BEING A HUMOROUS DESCRIPTION OF THE BAD BOY AND HIS DAD: IN THEIR JOURNEYS THROUGH FOREIGN LANDS - 1904
BY
George W. Peck

PECK'S BAD BOY ABROAD: BEING A HUMOROUS DESCRIPTION OF THE BAD BOY AND HIS DAD: IN THEIR JOURNEYS THROUGH FOREIGN LANDS - 1904

Published by Firework Press

New York City, NY

First published circa 1888

Copyright © Firework Press, 2015

All rights reserved

Except in the United States of America, this book is sold subject to the condition that it shall not, by way of trade or otherwise, be lent, re-sold, hired out, or otherwise circulated without the publisher's prior consent in any form of binding or cover other than that in which it is published and without a similar condition including this condition being imposed on the subsequent purchaser.

ABOUT FIREWORK PRESS

Firework Press prints and publishes the greatest books about American history ever written, including seminal works written by our nation's most influential figures.

CHAPTER I.

The bad boy had been away to school, but the illness of his father had called him home, and for some weeks he had been looking about the old town. He had found few of his old friends. His father had recovered somewhat from his illness, and one day he met his old chum, a boy of his own age. The bad boy and the chum got busy at once, talking over the old times that tried the souls of the neighbors and finally the bad boy asked about the old groceryman, and found that the old man still held out at the old stand, with the same old stock of groceries, and they decided to call upon him, and surprise him. So after it began to be dark they entered the store, and found the old groceryman sitting on a cracker box by the stove, stroking the back of an old maltese cat that had a yellow streak on the back, where it had been singed by crawling under the red-hot stove. As the boys entered the store the cat raised its back, its tail became as large as a rolling pin, and the cat began to spit, while the old groceryman held up both hands and said:

Don't Shoot, Please 019

"Don't shoot, please, but one of you go behind the counter and take what there is in the cash drawer, while the other one can reach into my pistol pocket and release my pocketbook. This is the fifth time I have been held up this year, and I have got so if I am not held up about so often I can't sleep nights."

"O, put down your hands and straighten out that cat's back," said the bad boy, as he slapped the old groceryman on the back so hard his spine cracked like a frozen sidewalk. "Don't you know us, you old geezer? We are the only and original Peck's Bad Boy and his Chum, come to life, and ready for business," and the two boys danced a jig on the floor, covered an inch thick with the spilled sugar of years ago, the molasses that had strayed from barrel, and the general refuse of the dirty place, which had become as hard as asphalt.

"O, dear, it is worse than I thought," said the old groceryman as he laughed a hysterical laugh through the long whiskers, and he hugged the boys as though he had a liking for them, notwithstanding the suffering they had caused him. "By gosh, I thought you were nothing but common robbers, who just wanted my money. You are old friends, and can have the whole place," and he poured some milk into a basin for the cat, but the animal only looked at the two boys as though she knew them, and watched them to see what was coming next.

The bad boy looked around the old grocery, which had not changed a particle during the time he had been away, the same old box of petrified prunes, the dried apples that could not be cut with a hatchet, the canned stuff on the shelves had become so old that the labels had curled up and fallen off, so it must have been a guess with the old groceryman whether he was selling a can of peas or tomatoes, and the old fellow standing there as though the world had gone off and left him, as his customers had.

"Well, wouldn't this skin you," said the bad boy, as he took up a dried prune and tried to crack it with a hatchet on a two-pound weight, turning to his chum who was stroking the singed hair of the old cat the wrong way. "Say, old man, you ought to get a hustle on you. Why don't you clean out this shebang, and put in a new stock, of goods, and have clerks with white aprons on, and a girl bookkeeper, and goods that people will buy and eat and not get sick? There is a grocery down street that is as clean as a whistle, and I notice all your old customers go there. Why don't you keep up with the times?"

"O, I ain't running a dude place," said the old man, as he took a piece of soft coal and put it in the old round stove, and wiped the black off his hands on his trousers. "I am trying to get rid of my customers. I have got money enough to live on, and I just stay here waiting for the old cat to die. I have only got six customers left, and one of them has got pneumonia, and is going to die, then there will be only five. When they are all gone I shall sit here by the stove until the end comes. There is nothing doing now to keep me awake, since you boys quit getting me mad. Say, boys, do you know, I haven't been real mad since you quit coming here. The only fun I have had is swearing at my customers when they stick up their noses at my groceries. It's the funniest thing, when I tell an old customer that if they don't like my goods they can go plum to thunder, they get mad and go somewhere else to trade. Times must be changing. Years ago, the more I abused customers the more they liked it, and I just charged the goods to them with a pencil on a piece of brown wrapping paper. I had four cracker boxes full of brown wrapping paper with things charged on the paper against customers, but when anybody wanted to pay their account it made my head ache to find it, and so one day I balanced my books by using the brown wrapping paper to kindle the fire. If you ever want to get even with the world, easy, just pour a little kerosene on your accounts, and put them in the stove. I have never been so free from worry as I have since I balanced my books in the stove. Well, I suppose you have come home on account of your dad's sickness," said the old groceryman, turning to the bad boy, who had written a sign, 'The Morgue,' and pinned it on the window. "I understand your dad had an operation performed on him in a hospital. What did the doctors take out of him?"

"Dad had an operation all right," said the bad boy, "but he is not as much interested in what they took out of him, as what he thinks they left in. They said they removed his appendix, and I guess they did, for dad showed me the bill the doctors rendered. The bill was big enough so they might have taken out a whole lot more. If I had been home I would never have let him be cut into, but ma insisted that he must have an operation. She said all the men on our street, and all that moved in our set, had had operations, and she was ashamed to go out in society and be forced to admit that dad never had an operation, She told dad that he could afford it better than half the people that had operations, and that a scar criss-cross on the stomach was a badge of honor. He never got a scar in the army, and she simply would not be able to look people in the face unless dad was operated on. Dad always was subject to stomach ache, but until appendicitis became fashionable he had always taken a mess of pills, and come out all right, but ma diagnosed the case the last time he was doubled up like a jack-knife, and dad was hustled off to the hospital, and they didn't do a thing to him.

"He told me about it since I came home, and now he lays the whole thing to ma, and I have to stand between them. He is going to get even with ma, though. The first time she complains of anything going on inside of her works, he is going to send her right to a hospital and have the doctors do their worst. Dad said to me, says he:

"'Hennery, if you ever feel anything like a caucus being held inside you, don't you ever go to a hospital, but just swallow a stick of dynamite and light the fuse, then there won't be anything left inside to bother you afterwards. When I got to the hospital they stripped me for a prize fight, put me on a table made of glass, and rolled me into the operating room, gave me chloroform and when they thought I was all in, they took an axe and chopped me. I could feel every blow, and it is a wonder they left enough of your old dad for you to hug when you came home.'

"Say, it is kind of pitiful to hear dad talk about the things they left in him."

"What things does he think they left in him," asked the old groceryman, as he looked frightened, and felt of his stomach, as though he mistrusted there might be something wrong with him, too.

"O, dad has been reading in the papers about doctors that perform operations leaving sponges, forceps, and things inside of patients, when they close up the place, and since dad has got pretty fussy since his operation he thinks they left something in him. Some days he thinks they left a roll of cotton batting, or a pillow, or a bale of hay, but when there is a sharp pain inside he thinks they left a carving knife, but for a week he has settled down to the belief that the doctors left a monkey wrench in him, and he is just daffy on that subject. Says he can feel it turning around, as though it was miscrewing machinery, and he wants to consult a new doctor every day as to what he can take to dissolve a monkey wrench, so it will pass off through the blood and pores of the skin. He has taken it into his head that nothing will save his life except to travel all over the country, and the world. I am to go with him to look after him."

Doctors Left a Monkey Wrench in Him 025

"By ginger, it's great! Just think of it. Traveling all over the world and nothing to do but nurse my old dad who thinks he is filled with hardware and carpenter's tools. Gee! but I wish you could go," said the bad boy, as he put him arm around his chum. "Maybe we wouldn't make these foreigners sit up and take an interest in something besides Royalty and Riots."

"Well," said the groceryman, "they will have my sympathy with you alone over there."

"But before you start on the road with your monkey-wrench show, you come in here and let me put up a package of those prunes to take along. They will keep in any climate, and there is nothing better for iron in the blood, such as your dad has, than prunes. Call again, bub, and we will arrange for you to write to your chum from all the places you go with your dad, and he can come in here and read the letters to me and the cat."

"All right, old Father Time," said the bad boy, as he drew a mug of cider out of the vinegar barrel, and took a swallow. "But what you want to do is to get a road scraper and drive a team through this grocery, and clean the floor," and the boys went out just ahead of the old man's arctic overshoes, as he kicked at them, and then he went back and sat down by the stove and stroked the cat, which had got its back down level again, after its old enemies had gone down the street, throwing snowballs at the driver of a hearse.

Went out Just Ahead of the Old Man's Arctic Overshoes 027

"It is a solemn occupation to drive a hearse," said the bad boy.

"Not so solemn as riding inside," said the chum.

CHAPTER II.

The old groceryman was in front of the grocery, bent over a box of rutabagas, turning the decayed sides down to make the possible customer think all was not as bad as it might be, when a shrill whistle down the street attracted his attention. He looked in the direction from which it came, and saw the bad boy coming with a suit case in one hand and a sole leather hat box in the other, and the old man went in the store to say a silent prayer, and to lay a hatchet and an ax handle where he could reach them if the worst came.

"Well, you want to get a good look at me now," said the bad boy, as he dropped the valise on the floor, and put the hat box on the counter, "for it will be months and maybe years, before you see me again."

"Oh, joy!" said the old groceryman, as he heaved a sigh, and tried to look sorry. "What is it, reform school, or have the police ordered you out of town? I have felt it coming for a long time. This is the only town you could have plied your vocation so long in and not been pulled. Where are you going with the dude suit case and the hat box?"

"Oh, dad has got a whole mess more diseases, and the doctors had a conversation over him Sunday, and they say he has got to go away again, right now, and that a sea voyage will brace him up and empty him out so medicine over in Europe can get in its work and strengthen him so he can start back after a while and probably die on the way home, and be buried at sea. Dad says he will go, for he had rather die at sea than on land, 'cause they don't have to have any trouble about a funeral, 'cause all they do is to sew a man up in a piece of cloth, tie a sack of coal to his feet, slide him off a board, and he goes kerplunk down into the salt water about a mile, and stands there on his feet and makes the whales and sharks think he is a new kind of fish."

"Gee! but that is a programme that appeals to me as sort of uncanny," said the old man. "Is your dad despondent over the outlook? What new disease has he got?"

Pasted a Tomato Can Label on the Suitcase 31

"All of 'em," said the boy, as he took a label off a tomato can and pasted it on the end of the suit case. "You take an almanac and read about all the diseases that the medicine advertised in the almanac cures, and dad has got the whole lot of them, nervous prostration, rheumatism, liver trouble, stomach busted, lungs congested, diaphragm turned over, heart disease, bronchitis, corns, bunions, every darn thing a man can catch without costing him anything. But he is not despondent. He just thinks it is an evidence of genius, and a certificate of standing in society and wealth. He argues that the poor people who have only one disease are not in it with statesmen and scholars. Oh, he is all right. He thinks if he goes to Europe all knocked out, he will class with emperors and dukes. Oh, since he had that operation and had his appendix chopped out, he thinks there is a bond of sympathy between him and King Edward that will cause him to be invited to be the guest of royalty. He is just daffy," and the bad boy took a sapolio label out of a box and pasted it on the other end of the valise.

"What in thunder and lightning are you pasting those labels on your valise for?" said the old man, as the boy reached for a Quaker oats label and a soap advertisement and pasted them on.

"Oh, dad said he wished he had some foreign labels of hotels and things on his valise, to make fellow travelers believe he had been abroad before, and I told him I could fix it all right. You see, if I paste things all over the valise he will think it is all right, 'cause he is near sighted," and the boy pasted on a label for 37 varieties of pickles, and then put on an advertisement for hair restorer on the hat box.

"Say, here's a fine one, this malted milk label, with a New Jersey cow on the corner," said the old man, as he began to take interest in the boy's talent as an artist. "And here, try one of these green pea can labels, and the pork and beans legend, and the only soap. Say, if you and your dad don't create a sensation from the minute you take the train till you get back, you can take it out of my wages. When are you going?"

"To-morrow night," said the boy, as he put more labels on the hat box, and stood off and looked at them with the eye of an artist. "We go to New York first to stay a few days and see things, and then we take a steamer and sail away, and the sicker dad is the more time I will have to fill up on useful nollig."

"Hennery," said the old groceryman, as his chin trembled, and a tear came to his eye. "I want to ask you a favor. At times, when you have been unusually mean, I have thought I hated you, but when I have said something ugly to you, and have laid awake all night regretting it, it has occurred to me that you were about the best friend I had. I think it makes an old man forget his years, to be chummy with a live boy, full of ginger, and I do like you, condemn you, and I can't help it. Now I want you to write me every little while, on your trip, and I will read your letters to the customers here in the store, who will be lonely until they can hear that you are dead. The neighbors will come in to read your letters, and it will bring me custom. Will you write to me, boy, and pour out your heart to me, and tell me of the different troubles you get your dad into, for surely you cannot help finding trouble over there if you go hunting for it. Promise me, boy."

"You bet your life I will, old pard," said the bad boy. "I shall have to have some escape valve to keep from busting. I was going to write to my chum, but he is in love with a telephone girl, and he don't take any time for pleasure. I will write you about every dutch and duchess we meet, every prince and pauper, and everything. You watch my smoke, and you will think there is a train afire. I hope dad will try and restrain himself from wanting to fight everybody that belongs to any country but America. He has bought one one these little silk American flags to wear in his button hole, and he swears if anybody looks cross-eyed at that flag he will simply cut his liver out, and toast it on a fork, and eat it. He makes me tired, and I know there is going to be trouble."

"Don't you think your dad's mind sort of wanders?" said the old groceryman, in a whisper, "It wouldn't be strange, after all he has gone through, in raising you up to your present size, if he was a little off his base."

"Well, ma thinks he is bug-house, and the hired girl is willing to go into court and swear to it, and that experience we had coming home from the Yellowstone park some time ago, made me think if he was not crazy he would be before long, You see, we had a hot box on the engine, and had to stay at a station in the bad lands for an hour, and there were a mess of cow boys on the platform, and I told dad we might as well have some amusement while we were there, and that a brake-man told me the cow boys were great dancers, but you couldn't hire them to dance, but if some man with a strong personality would demand that they dance, and put his hand on his pistol pocket they would all jump in and dance for an hour. That was enough for dad, for he has a microbe that he is a man of strong personality, and that when he demands that anybody do something they simply got to do it, so he walked up and down the platform a couple of times to get his draw poker face on, and I went up to one of the cow boys and told him that the old duffer used to be a ballet dancer, and he thought everybody ought to dance when they were told to, and that if the spell should come on him, and he should order them to dance, it would be a great favor to me if they would just give him a double shuffle or two, just to ease his mind.

"Well, pretty soon he came along to where the cowboys were leaning against the railing, and, looking at them in a haughty manner, he said: 'Dance, you kiotes, dance,' and he put his hand to his pistol pocket. Well, sir, I never saw so much fun in my life. Four of the cow boys pulled revolvers and began to shoot regular bullets into the platform within an inch of dad's feet, and they yelled to him: 'Dance your own self, you ancient maverick; whoop 'er up!' and by gosh! dad was so frightened that he began to dance all around the platform, and it was like a battle, the bullets splintering the boards, and the smoke filling the air, and the passengers looking out of the windows and laughing, and the engineer and fireman looking on and yelling, and dad nearly exhausted from the exertion. I guess if the conductor had not got the hot box put out and yelled all aboard, dad would have had apoplexy."

He Began to Dance All Around the Platform 037

"When he let up, the cow boys quit shooting, and he!'ol aboard the train and started. I stayed in the smoking car with the train butcher for more than an hour, 'cause I was afraid if I went in the car where dad was he would make some remark that would offend my pride, and when I did go back to the car he just said: 'Somebody fooled you. Those fellows couldn't dance, and I knew it all the time.' Yes, I guess there is no doubt dad is crazy sometimes, but let me chaperone him through a few foreign countries and he will stand without hitching all right. Well, goodby, now, old man, and try and bear up under it, till you get a letter from me," and the bad boy took his labeled valise and hat box and started.

CHAPTER III.

Washington, D. C—My Dear Old Skate: I didn't tell you in my last about the fun we had getting here. We were on the ocean wave two days, because the whole country was flooded from the rains, and dad walked the quarter deck of the Pullman car, and hitched up his pants, and looked across the sea on each side of the train with a field glass, looking for whales and porpoises. He seems to be impressed with the idea that this trip abroad is one of great significance to the country, and that he is to be a sort of minister plenipotentiary, whatever that is, and that our country is going to be judged by the rest of the world by the position he takes on world affairs. The first day out of Chicago dad corraled the porter in a section and talked to him until the porter was black in the face. I told dad the only way to get respectful consideration from a negro was to advocate lynching and burning at the stake, for the slightest things, so when our porter was unusually attentive to a young woman on the car dad hauled him over the coals, and scared him so by talking of hanging, and burning in kerosene oil, that the negro got whiter than your shirt, and when he got away from dad he came to me and asked if that old man with the red nose and the gold-headed cane was as dangerous as he talked. I told him he was my dad, and that he was a walking delegate of the Amalgamated Association of Negro Lynchers, and when a negro did anything that he ought to be punished for they sent for dad, and he took charge of the proceedings and saw that the negro was hanged, and shot, and burned up plenty. But I told him that dad was crazy on the subject of giving tips to servants, and he must not fall dead when we got to Washington if dad gave him a $50 bill, and he must not give back any change, but just act as though he always got $50 from passengers. Well, you'd a dide to see that negro brush dad 50 times a day, and bring a towel every few minutes to wipe off his shoes, but he kept one eye,' about as big as an onion, on dad all the time, to watch that he didn't get stabbed. The next morning I took dad's pants from under his pillow, and hid them in a linen closet, and dad laid in his berth all the forenoon, and had it out with the porter, whom he accused of stealing them. The doctors told me I must keep dad interested and excited, so he would not dwell on his sickness, and I did, sure as you are a foot high. Dad stood it till almost noon, when he came out of his berth with his pajamas on, these kind with great blue stripes like a fellow in the penitentiary, and when he went to the wash room I found his pants and then he dressed up and swore some at everybody but me. We got to Washington all right, and I thought I would bust when dad fished out a nickel and gave it to the porter, and we got out of the car before the porter came to, and the first day we stayed in the hotel for fear the negro would see us, as I told dad that porter would round up a gang of negroes with razors and they would waylay us and cut dad all up into sausage meat.

Fished out a Nickel and Gave It to the Porter

Dad is the bravest man I ever saw when there is no danger, but when there is a chance for a row he is weak as a cat. I spect it is on account of his heart being weak. A man's internal organs are a great study. I spose a brave man, a hero, has to have all his inside things working together, to be real up and up brave, but if his heart is strong, and his liver is white, he goes to pieces in an emergency, and if his liver is all right, and he tries to fight just on his liver, when the supreme moment arrives, and his heart jumps up into his throat, and wabbles and beats too quick, he just flunks. I would like to dissect a real brave man, and see what condition the things inside him are in, but it would be a waste of time to dissect dad, 'cause I know all his inner works need to go to a watchmaker and be cleaned, and a new main spring put in.

  Well, this morning dad shaved himself, and got on his frock coat, and his silk hat, and said we would go over to the white house and have a talk with Teddy, but first he wanted to go and see where Jefferson hitched his horse to the fence when he came to Washington to be innogerated, and where Jackson smoked his corn cob pipe, and swore and stormed around when he was mad, and to walk on the same paths where Zachariah Taylor Zacked, Buchanan catched it, and Lincoln put down the rebellion, and so we walked over toward the white house, and I was scandalized. I stopped to pick up a stone to throw at a dog inside the fence, and when I walked along behind dad, and got a rear view of his silk hat, it seemed as though I would sink through the asphalt pavement, for he had on an old silk hat that he wore before the war, the darnedest looking hat I ever saw, the brim curled like a minstrel show hat, the fur rubbed off in some places, and he looked like one of these actors that you see pictures of walking on the railroad track, when the show busts up at the last town. I think a man ought to dress so his young son won't have a fit. I tried to get dad to go and buy a new hat, but he said he was going to wait till he got to London, and buy one just like King Edward wears, but he will never get to London with that hat, 'cause to-night I will throw it out of the hotel window and put a piece of stove pipe in his hat box.

  Well, sir, you wouldn't believe it, but we got into the white house without being pulled, but it was a close shave, 'cause everybody looked at dad, and put their forefingers to their foreheads, for they thought he was either a crank, or an ambassador from some furrin country. The detectives got around dad when we got into the anteroom, and began to feel of his pockets to see if he had a gun, and one of them asked me what the old fellow wanted, and I told them he was the greatest bob cat shooter in the west, and was on his way to Europe to invite the emperors and things to come over to this country and shoot cats on his preserve. Well, say, you ought to have seen how they stepped one side and waltzed around, and one of them went in the next room and told the president dad was there, and before we knew it we were in the president's room, and the president began to curl up his lip, and show his teeth like some one had said "rats."

President Began to Curl up his Lip 045

  He got hold of dad's hand, and dad backed off as though he was afraid of being bitten, and then they sat down and talked about mountain lion and cat shooting, and dad said he had a 22 rifle that he could pick a cat off the back fence with every time, out of his bedroom window, and I began to look around at the pictures. Dad and the president talked about all kinds of shooting, from mudhens to moose, and then dad told the president he was going abroad on account of his liver, and wanted a letter of introduction to some of the kings and emperors, and queens, and jacks, and all the face cards, and the president said he made it a practice not to give any personal letters to his friends, the kings, but that dad could tell any of them that he met that he was an

American citizen, and that would take him anywhere in Europe, and then he got up and began to show his teeth at dad again, and dad gave him the grand hailing sign of distress of the Grand Army and backed out, dropped his hat, and in trying to pick it up, he stepped on it, but that made it look better, anyway, and we found ourselves outside the room, and a lot of common people from the country were ready to go in and talk politics and cat shooting.

Well, we looked at pictures, and saw the state dining room where they feed 50 diplomats at a time on mud turtle and champagne, and a boy about my size looked sort of disdainful at me, and I told him it he would come outside I would mash his jaw, and he said I could try it right there if I was in a hurry to go, and I was starting to give him a swift punch when a detective took hold of my arm and said they couldn't have any scrap there, 'cause the president's son could not fight with common boys, and I asked him who he called a common boy, and then dad said we better go before war broke out in a country that was illy prepared for hostilities on a large scale, and then I told a detective that dad was liable to have one of his spells and begin shooting any minute, and then the detectives all thought dad was one of these president assassinationists, and they took him into a room and searched him, and asked him a whole lot of fool questions, and they finally let us out, and told us we better skip the town before night.

I Was Starting to Give Him a Swift Punch 047

Dad got kind of heavy-hearted over that and took a notion he would like to see ma again before crossing the briny deep, so you came near having your little angel again soon. This weakness of dad's didn't last long, for we're looking for a warm time in New York and old Lunnon.

So long,

Hennery.

CHAPTER IV.

New York City.—My Dear Uncle Ezra: I got a letter from my chum this morning, and he says he was in the grocery the day he wrote, and you were a sight. He says that if I am going to be away several months you will never change your shirt till I get back, for nobody around the grocery seems to have any influence over you. I meant to have put you under bonds before I left, to change your shirt at least quarterly, but you ought to change it by rights every month. The way to do is to get an almanac and make a mark on the figures at the first of the month, and when you are studying the almanac it will remind you of your duty to society. People east here, that is, business men in your class, change their shirts every week or two. Try and look out for these little matters, insignificant as they may seem, because the public has some rights that it is dangerous for a man to ignore.

Dad and I have been down to Mount Vernon, and had a mighty solemn time. I think dad expected that we would be met at the trolley car by a delegation of descendants of George Washington, by a four-horse carriage, with postilions and things, and driven to the old house, and received with some distinction, as dad had always been an admirer of George Washington, and had pointed with pride to his record as a statesman and a soldier, but all we saw was a bunch of negroes, who told us which way to walk, and charged us ten cents apiece for the information.

At Mount Vernon we found the old house where George lived and died, where Martha told him to wipe his feet before he came in the house, and saw that things were cooked properly. We saw pictures of revolutionary scenes and men of that period, relics of the days when George was the whole thing around there. We saw the bed on which George died, and then we went down to the icehouse and looked through the fence and saw the marble coffins in which George and Martha were sealed up. Say, old man, I know you haven't got much reverence, but you couldn't look through that fence at what remains of the father of his country without taking off your hat and thinking good things while you were there.

Saw the Marble Coffins in Which George and Martha 050

I was surprised at dad; he cried, though he never met George Washington in all his life. I have seen dad at funerals at home, when he was a bearer, or a mourner, and he never acted as thought it affected him much, but there at Mount Vernon, standing within eight feet of the remains of George Washington, he just lost his nerve, and bellered, and I felt solemn myself, like I had been kept in after school when all the boys were going in swimming. If a negro had not asked dad for a quarter I know dad would have got down on his knees and been pious, but when he gave that negro a swift kick for butting in with a commercial proposition, in a sacred moment, dad come to, and we went up to the house again. Dad said what he wanted was to think of George Washington just as a country farmer, instead of a general and a president. He said we got nearer to George, if we thought of him getting up in the morning, putting on his old farmer pants and shirt, and going downstairs in his stocking feet, and going out to the kitchen by the wooden bench, dipping a gourd full of rain water out of a barrel into an earthen wash basin and taking some soft soap out of a dish and washing himself, his shirt open so his great hairy breast would catch the breeze, his suspenders, made of striped bed ticking, hanging down, his hair touseled up until he had taken out a yellow pocket comb and combed it, and then yelling to Martha to know about how long a workingman would have to wait for breakfast. And then dad said he liked to think of George Washington sitting down at the breakfast table and spearing sausages out of a platter, and when a servant brought in a mess of these old-fashioned buckwheat cakes, as big as a pieplate, see George, in imagination, pilot a big one on to his plate, and cover it with sausage gravy, and eat like he didn't have any dyspepsia, and see him help Martha to buckwheat cakes, and finally get up from breakfast like a full Christian and go out on the farm and count up the happy slaves to see if any of them had got away during the night.

By ginger, dad inspired me with new thoughts about the father of his country. I had always thought of Washington as though he was constantly crossing the Delaware in a skiff, through floating ice, with a cocked hat on, and his coat flaps trimmed with buff nankeen stuff, a sort of a male Eliza in "Uncle Tom's Cabin," getting away from the hounds that were chasing her to chew her pants. I was always thinking of George either chopping cherry trees, or standing on a pedestal to have his picture taken, but here at the old farm, with dad to inspire me, I was just mingling with Washington, the planter, the neighbor, telling the negroes where they would get off at if they didn't pick cotton fast enough, or breaking colts, or going to the churn and drinking a quart of buttermilk, and getting the stomach ache, and calling upstairs to Martha, who was at the spinning wheel, or knitting woolen socks, and asking her to fix up a brandy smash to cure his griping pains. I thought of the father of his country taking a severe cold, and not being able to run into a drug store for a bottle of cough sirup, or a quinine pill, having Martha fix a tub of hot mustard water to soak those great feet of his, and bundle him up in a flannel blanket, give him a hot whisky, and put him to bed with a hot brick at his feet.

Then, when I looked at a duck blind out in the Potomac, near the shore, I thought how George used to put on an old coat and slouch hat and take his gun and go out in the blind, and shoot canvas-back ducks for dinner, and paddle his boat out after the dead birds, the way Grover Cleveland did a century later. I tell you, old man, the way to appreciate our great statesmen, soldiers and scholars is to think of them just as plain, ordinary citizens, doing the things men do nowadays. It does dad and I more good to think of Washington and his friends camping out down the Potomac, on a fishing trip, sleeping on a bed of pine boughs, and cooking their own pork, and roasting sweet potatoes in the ashes, eating with appetites like slaves, than to think of him at a state dinner in the white house, with a French cook disguising the food so they could not tell what it was.

O, I had rather have a picture of George Washington and Lafayette coming up the bank of the Potomac toward the house, loaded down with ducks, and Martha standing on the porch of Mount Vernon asking them who they bought the ducks of and how much they cost, than to have one of those big paintings in the white house showing George and Lafayette looking as though they had conquered the world. If the phonograph had been invented then, and we could listen to the conversation of those men, just as they said things, it would be great. Imagine George saying to Lafayette, so you cotild hear it now: "Lafe, that last shot at that canvasback you made was the longest shot ever made on the Potomac. It was a Jim dandy, you old frog eater," and imagine Lafayette replying: "You bet your life, George, I nailed that buck canvasback with a charge of number six shot, and he never knew what struck him." But they didn't have any phonographs in those days and so you have got to imagine things.

How would Washington's farewell address sound now in a phonograph, or some of George's choice swear words at a slave that had ridden a sore-backed mule down to Alexandria after a jug of rum. I would like to run a phonograph show with nothing in the machine but ancient talk from George Washington, but we can have no such luck unless George is born again.

Old man, if you ever get a furlough from business, you go down to Mount Vernon and revel in memories of the father of his country. If you go, hunt up a negro with a hair lip, that is a servant there, and who used to be Washington's body servant, unless he is a liar, and tell him I sent you and he won't do a thing to you, for a dollar or so. I told that negro that dad was a great general, a second Washington, and he wore all the skin off his bald head taking off his hat to dad every time dad looked at him, and he bowed until his back ached, but when we were going away, and dad asked me what ailed the old monkey to act that way, the old negro thought these new Washingtons were a pretty tough lot.

All the time at Mount Vernon I couldn't get up meanness enough to play any trick on dad, but I picked up a sort of a horse chestnut or something, with prickers on it as sharp as needles, and as we were getting on the trolley I slipped it down the back of dad's pants, near where his suspenders button on, and by the time we sat down in the car the horse chestnut had worked down where dad is the largest, and when he leaned back against the seat he turned pale and wiggled around and asked me if he looked bad.

Slipped It Down the Back of Dad's Pants 057

I told him he looked like a corpse, which encouraged him so he almost fainted. He asked me if I had heard of any contagious diseases that were prevalent in Virginia, 'cause he felt as though he had caught something. I told him I would ask the conductor, so I went and asked the conductor what time we got to Washington, and then I went back to dad and told him the conductor said there was no disease of any particular account, except smallpox and yellow fever, and that the first symptom of smallpox was a prickling sensation in the small of the back.

Dad turned green and said he had got it all right, and I had the darndest time getting him back to the hotel at Washington. Say, I had to help him undress, and I took the horse chestnut and put it in the foot of the bed, and got dad in, and I went downstairs to see a doctor, and then I came back and told him the doctor said if the prickly sensation went to his feet he was in no danger from smallpox, as it was an evidence that an old vaccination of years ago had got in its work and knocked the disease out of his system lengthwise, and when I told dad that he raised up in bed and said he was saved, for ever since I went out of the room he had felt that same dreaded prickling at work on his feet, and he was all right.

I told dad it was a narrow escape and that it ought to be a warning to him. Dad has to wear a dress suit to dinner here and cough up money every time he turns around, 'cause I have told the bell boys dad is a bonanza copper king, and they are not doing a thing to dad.

O, I guess I am doing just as the doctors at home ordered, in keeping dad's mind occupied.

Well, so long, old man, I have got to go to dinner with dad, and I am going to order the dinner myself, dad said I could, and if I don't put him into bankruptcy, you don't know your little Hennery.

CHAPTER V.

Waldorf-Astoria, New York.—Dear Uncle Ezra: We are still at this tavern, but we don't do anything but sleep here, and stay around in the lobby evenings to let people look at us, and dad wears that old swallow-tail coat he had before the war, but he has got a new silk hat, since we got here; one of these shiny ones that is so slick it makes his clothes look offul bum. We about went broke on the first supper we had, or dinner they call it here. You see, dad thought this was about a three-dollar-a-day house, and that the meals were included, like they do at Oshkosh, and so when we went down to dinner dad said we wouldn't do a thing to old Astor. He let me order the dinner, but told me to order everything on the bill-of-sale, because we wanted to get the worth of our three dollars a day. Well, honest, I couldn't order all there was, 'cause you couldn't have got it all on a billiard table. Say, that list they gave me had everything on it that was ever et or drunk, but I told dad they would fire us out if we ordered the whole prescription, so all I ordered was terrapin, canvasback duck, oysters, clams, crabs, a lot of new kinds of fish, and some beef and mutton, and turkey, and woodcock, and partridge, and quail, and English pheasant, and lobster and salads and ices, and pie and things, just to stay our stomachs, and when it came to wine, dad weakened, because he didn't want to set a bad example to me, so he ordered hard cider for hisself and asked me if I wanted anything to drink, and I ordered brown pop. You'd a been tickled to see the waiter when he took that order, 'cause I don't s'pose anybody ever ordered cider and brown pop there since Astor skinned muskrats for a living, when he was a trapper up north. Gosh, but when they brought that dinner in, you ought to have seen the sensation it created. Most of the people in the great dining hall looked at dad as though he was a Crases, or a Rockefeller, and the head waiter bowed low to dad, and dad thought it was Astor, and dad looked dignified and hurt at being spoken to by a common tavern keeper. Well, we et and et, but we couldn't get away with hardly any of it, and dad wanted to wrap some of the duck and lobsters and things in a newspaper and take it to the room for a lunch, but the waiter wouldn't have it. But the cyclone struck the house when dad and I got up to go out of the dining-room, and the waiter brought dad the check.

The Waiter Brought Dad the Check 063

"What is this?" said dad, as he put on his glasses and looked at the check which was $43 and over.

"Dinner check, sir," said the waiter, as he straightened back and held out his hand.

"Why, ain't this house run on the American plan?" said dad, as his chin began to tremble.

"No, sir, on the Irish plan," said the waiter. "You pays for what you horders," and dad began to dig up. He looked at me as though I was to blame, when he told me to order all there was in sight. Well, I have witnessed heart-rending scenes, but I never saw anything that would draw tears like dad digging down for that $43. The doctors at home had ordered excitement for dad, but this seemed to be an overdose, and I was afraid he would collapse and I offered him my glass of brown pop to stimulate him, but he told me I could go plumb, and if I spoke to him again he would maul me. He got his roll half out of his pistol pocket, and then talked loud and said it was a damoutridge, and he wanted to see Astor himself before he would allow himself to be held up by highwaymen, and then all the other diners stood up and looked at dad, and a lot of waiters and bouncers surrounded him, and then he pulled out the roll, and it was pitiful to see him wet his trembling thumb on his trembling dry tongue and begin to peel off the bills, like you peel the layers off an onion, but he got off enough to pay for the dinner, gave the waiter half a dollar, and smiled a sickly smile at the head waiter, and I led him out of the dining-room a broken-down old man. As we got to the lobby, where the horse show of dress-suit chappies was beginning the evening procession, I said to dad: "Next time we will dine out, I guess," and at that he rallied and seemed to be able to take a joke, for he said: "We dined out this time. We dined out $43," and then we joined the procession of walkers around, and tried to look prosperous, and after awhile dad called a bell boy, and asked him if there wasn't a good dairy lunch counter near the Waldorf, where a man could go and get a bowl of bread and milk, and the bell boy gave him the address of a dairy lunch place, and I can see my finish, 'cause from this out we will probably live on bread and milk while we are here, and I hate bread and milk.

It got all around the hotel, about the expensive dinner dad ordered for himself and the little heir to his estate, and everybody wanted to get acquainted with dad and try to get some stock in his copper mine. I had told dad about my telling the boys he was a bonanza copper miner, and he never batted an eye when they asked him about his mine, and he looked the part.

One Man Wanted Dad to Cash a Check 067

One man wanted dad to cash a check, 'cause the bank was closed, and he was a rich-looking duke, and dad was just going to get his roll out and peel off some more onion, when I said: "Not on your tintype, Mr. Duke," and dad left his roll in his pocket, and the duke gave me a look as though he wanted to choke me, and went away, saying: "There is Mr. Pierpont Morgan, and I can get him to cash it." I saved dad over a hundred dollars on that scheme, and so we are making money every minute. We went to our room early, so dad could digest his $43 worth of glad food.

Gee, but this house got ripped up the back before morning. You remember I told you about a countess, or a duchess, or some kind of high-up female that had a room next to our room. Well, she is a beaut, from Butte, Mont., or Cuba, or somewhere, for she acts like a queen that has just stepped off her throne for a good time. She has got a French maid that is a peacharino. You know that horse chestnut, with the prickers on, that I put in dad's pants at Washington. Well, I have still got it, and as it gets dry the prickers are sharper than needles, sharper even than a servant's tooth, as it says in the good book. I thought I would give dad a run for his money, 'cause exercise and excitement are good for a man that dined heartily on $43 worth of rich food, so when we went to our room I told dad that I was satisfied from what a bell boy told me that the countess in the next room, who had gold cords over her shoulders for suspenders, was stuck on him, because she was always inquiring who the lovely old gentleman was with the sweet little boy. Dad he got so interested that he forgot to cuss me about ordering that dinner, and he said he had noticed her, and would like real well to get acquainted with her, 'cause a man far away from home, sick as a dog, with no loving wife to look after him, needed cheerful company. So I told him I had it all arranged for him to meet her, and then I went out in the hall, sort of whistling around, and the French maid came out and broke some English for me, and we got real chummy, 'cause she was anxious to learn English, and I wanted to learn some French words; so she invited me into the room, and we sat on the sofa and exchanged words quite awhile, until she was called to the telephone in the other room. Say, you ought to have seen me. I jumped up and put my hand inside the sheets of the bed, and put that chestnut in there, right about the middle of the bed, and then, after learning French quite a spell, with the maid, we heard the countess getting off the elevator, and the maid said I must skip, 'cause it was the countess' bed-time, and I went back and told dad the whole thing was arranged for him to meet the countess, in a half an hour or so, as she had to write a few letters to some kings and dukes, and when she gave a little scream; as though she was practicing her voice on an opera, or something, dad was to go and rap at the door. Gosh, but I was sorry for dad, for he was so nervous and anxious for the half hour to expire that he walked up and down the room, and looked at himself in the mirror, and acted like he had indigestion. I had told the maid that she and the countess must feel perfectly safe, if anything ever happened, 'cause my dad was the bravest man in the world, and he would rush to the rescue of the countess, if a burglar got in in the night, or the water pipes busted, or anything, and all she had to do was to screech twice and dad would be on deck, and she must open the door quicker-n scat, and she thanked me, and said she would, and for me to come, too. Say, on the dead, wasn't that a plot for an amateur to cook up? Well, sir, we had to wait so long for the countess to get on the horse chestnut that I got nervous myself, but after awhile there came a scream that would raise your hair, and I told dad the countess was singing the opera. Dad said: "Hennery, that ain't no opera, that's tragedy," but she gave two or three more stanzas, and I told dad he better hustle, and we went out in the hall and rapped at the door of the countess' room, and the maid opened it, and told us to send for a doctor and a policeman, 'cause the countess was having a fit. Well, say, that was the worst ever. The countess had jumped out of bed, and was pulling the lace curtains around her, but dad thought she was crazy, and was going to jump out of the window, and he made a grab for her, and he shouted to her to "be cam, be cam, poor woman, and I will rescue you." I tried to pacify the maid the best I knew how, and dad was getting the countess calmer, but she evidently thought he was an assassin, for every little while she would yell for help, and then the night watchman came in with a house policeman, and one of them choked dad off, and they asked the countess what the trouble was, and she said she had just retired when she was stabbed about a hundred times in the small of the back with a poniard, and she knew conspirators were assassinating her, and she screamed, and this old bandit, meaning dad, came in, and the little monkey, meaning me, had held his hand over her maid's mouth, so she could not make any outcry.

Night Watchman Came in With a House Policeman

Well, I got my horse chestnut all right, out of the bed, and the policeman told the countess not to be alarmed, and go back to bed, and they took dad and I to our room, and asked us all about it. Gee, but dad put up a story about hearing a woman scream in the next room, and, thinking only of the duty of a gentleman under the circumstances, rushed to her rescue, and all there was to it was that she must have had a nightmare, but he said if he had it to do over again, he would do the same. Anyway, the policeman believed dad, and they went off and left us, and we went to bed, but dad said: "Hennery, you understand, I don't want to make any more female acquaintances, see, among the crowned heads, and from this out we mingle only with men. The idea of me going into a woman's room and finding a Floradora with fits and tantrums, and me, a sick man. Now, don't write to your ma about this, 'cause she never did have much confidence in me, around women with fits." So, Uncle Ezra, you must not let this get into the papers, see?

Well, we have bought our tickets for Liverpool, and shall sail to-morrow, and while you are making up your cash account Saturday night, we shall be on the ocean. I s'pose I will write you on the boat, if they will tie it up somewhere so it will stand level. Your dear boy. Hennery.

CHAPTER VI.

On Board the Lucinia, Mid-ocean.
Dear Old Geezer.
I take the first opportunity, since leaving New York, to write you, 'cause the boat, after three days out, has got settled down so it runs level, and I can write without wrapping my legs around the table legs, to hold me down. I have tried a dozen times to write, but the sea was so rough that part of the time the table was on top of me and part of the time I was on top, and I was so sick I seem to have lost my mind, over the rail, with the other things supposed to be inside of me. O, old man, you think you know what seasickness is, 'cause you told me once about crossing Lake Michigan on a peach boat, but lake sickness is easy compared with the ocean malady. I could enjoy common seasickness and think it was a picnic, but this salt water sickness takes the cake. I am sorry for dad, because he holds more than I do, and he is so slow about giving up meals that he has paid for, that it takes him longer to commune with nature, and he groans so, and swears some.

I Am Sorry for Dad, Because he Holds More Than I Do 074

I don't see how a person can swear when he is seasick on the ocean, with no sure thing that he will ever see land again, and a good prospect of going to the bottom, where you got to die in the arms of a devil fish, with a shark biting pieces out of your tender loin and a smoked halibut waiting around for his share of your corpse, and whales blowing syphons of water and kicking because they are so big that they can't get at you to chew cuds of human gum, and porpoises combing your damp hair with their fine tooth comb fins, and sword fish and sawtooth piscatorial carpenters sawing off steaks. Gee, but it makes me crawl. I once saw a dead dog in the river, with bull heads and dog-fish ripping him up the back, and I keep thinking I had rather be that dog, in a nice river at home, with bullheads that I knew chewing me at their leisure, than to be a dead boy miles down in the ocean, with strange fish and sea serpents quarreling over the tender pieces in me. A man told me that if you smoke cigarets and get saturated with nickoteen, and you are drownded, the fish will smell of you, and turn up their noses and go away and leave your remains, so I tried a cigaret, and, gosh, but I had rather be et by fish than smoke another, on an ocean steamer. It only added to my sickness, and I had enough before. I prayed some, when the boat stood on its head and piled us all up in the front end, but a chair struck me on the place where Fitzsimmons hit Corbett, and knocked the prayer all out of me, and when the boat stood on her butt end and we all slid back the whole length of the cabin, and I brought up under the piano, I tried to sing a hymn, such as I used to in the 'Piscopal choir, before my voice changed, but the passengers who were alive yelled for some one to choke me, and I didn't sing any more. Dad was in the stateroom when we were rolling back and forth in the cabin, and between sicknesses he came out to catch me and take me into the stateroom, but he got the rolling habit, too, and he rolled a match with an actress who was voyaging for her health, and they got offully mixed up. He tried to rescue her, and grabbed hold of her belt and was reeling her in all right, when a man who said he was her husband took dad by the neck and said he must keep his hands off or get another nose put on beside the one he had, and then they all rolled under a sofa, and how it came out I don't know, but the next morning dad's eye was blacked, and the fellow who said he was her husband had his front teeth knocked out, and the actress lost her back hair and had to wear a silk handkerchief tied around her head the rest of the trip, and she looked like a hired girl who has been out to a saloon dance.

    The trouble with dad is that he butts in too much. He thinks he is the whole thing and thinks every crowd he sees is a demonstration for him. When the steamer left New York, there were hundreds of people on the dock to see friends off, and they had flowers to present to Unfriends, and dad thought they were all for him, and he reached for every bunch of roses that was brought aboard, and was going to return thanks for them, when they were jerked away from him, and he looked hurt. When the gang plank was pulled in, and the boat began to wheeze, and grunt, and move away from the dock, and dad saw the crowd waving handkerchiefs and laughing, and saying bon voyage, he thought they were doing it all for him, and he started in to make a speech, thanking his fellow countrymen for coming to see him off, and promising them that he would prove a true representative of his beloved country in his travels abroad, and that he would be true to the stars and stripes wherever fortune might place him, and all that rot, when the boat got so far away they could not hear him, and then he came off his perch, and said, "Hennery, that little impromptu demonstration to your father, on the eve of his departure from his native land, perhaps never to return, ought to be a deep and lasting lesson to you, and to show you that the estimation in which I am held by our people, is worth millions to you, and you can point with pride to your father." I said "rats" and dad said he wouldn't wonder if the boat was full of rats, and then we stood on deck, and watched the objects of interest down the bay.

A Speech, Thanking his Fellow Countrymen 078

As we passed the statue of Liberty, which France gave to the republic, on Bedloe's Island, dad started to make a speech to the passengers, but one of the officers of the boat told dad this was no democratic caucus, and that choked him off, but he was loaded for a speech, and I knew it was only a matter of time when he would have to fire it off, but I thought when we got outside the bar, into the ocean, his speech would come up with the rest of the stuff, and I guess it did, for after he began to be sea sick he had to keep his mouth shut, which was a great relief to me, for I felt that he would say something that would get this country in trouble with other nations, as there were lots of foreigners on board. I heard that J. Pierpont Morgan was on board, and I told everybody I got in conversation with that dad was Pierpont Morgan, and when people began to call him Mr. Morgan, I told dad the passengers thought he was Morgan; the great financier, and it tickled dad, and he never denied it. Anyway, the captain put dad and I at his own table, and he called me "Little Pierp," and everybody discussed great financial questions with dad, and everything would have been lovely the whole trip, only Morgan came amongst us after he had been sea sick for three days, and they gave him a seat opposite us, and with two Morgans at the same table it was a good deal like two Uncle Tom's in an Uncle Tom's Cabin show, so dad had to stay in his stateroom on account of sickness, a good deal. Then dad got to walking on deck and flirting with the female passengers. Say, did you ever see an old man who was stuck on hisself, and thought that every woman who looked at him, from curiosity, or because he had a wart on his neck, and watch him get busy making 'em believe he is a young and kitteny thing, who is irresistible? Gee, but it makes me tired. No man can mash, and make eyes, and have a love scene, when he has to go to the rail every few minutes and hump hisself with something in him that is knocking at the door of his palate, to come out the same way it went in. Dad found a widow woman who looked back at him kind of sassy, when he braced up to her, and when the ship rolled and side-stepped, he took hold of her arm to steady her, and she said maybe they better sit down on deck and talk it over, so dad found a couple of steamer chairs that were not in use, and they sat down near together, and dad took hold of her hand to see if she was nervous, and he told me I could go any play mumbletypeg in the cabin, and I went in the cabin and looked out of the window at dad and the widow. Say, you wouldn't think two chairs could get so close, and dad was sure love sick, and so was she. The difference between love sick and sea sick is that in love sick you look red in the face and snuggle up, and squeeze hands, and look fondly, and swallow your emotion, and try to wait patiently until it is dark enough so the spectators won't notice anything, and in sea sickness you get pale in the face, and spread apart, and let go of hands, and after you have stood it as long as you can you rush to the rail and act as though you were going to jump overboard, and then stop sudden and let-'er-go-gallagher, right before folks, and after it is over you try to look as though you had enjoyed it. I will say this much for dad, he and the widow never played a duet over the rail, but they took turns, and dad held her as tenderly as though they were engaged, and when he got her back to the steamer chair he stroked her face and put camphor to her nose, and acted like an undertaker that wasn't going to let the remains get away from him. They were having a nice convalescent time, just afore it broke up, and hadn't either of them been sick for ten minutes, and dad had put his arm around her shoulders, and was talking cunning to her, and she was looking lovingly into dad's eyes, and they were talking of meeting again in France in a few weeks, where she was going to rent a villa, and dad was saying he would be there with both feet, when I opened the window and said, "The steward is bringing around a lunch, and I have ordered two boiled pork sandwiches for you two easy marks." Well, you'd a dide to see 'em jump. What there is about the idea of fat pork that makes people who are sea sick have a relapse, I don't know, but the woman grabbed her stum-mix in both hands and left dad and rushed into the cabin yelling "enough," or something like that, and dad laid right back in the chair and blatted like a calf, and said he would kill me dead when we got ashore. Just then an Englishman came along and told dad he better get up out of his chair, and dad said whose chair you talking about, and the man said the chair was his, and if dad didn't get out of it, he would kick him in the pants, and dad said he hadn't had a good chance at an Englishman since the Revolutionary war, and he just wanted a chance to clean up enough Englishmen for a mess, and dad got up and stood at "attention," and the Englishman squared off like a prize fighter, and they were just going to fight the battle of Bunker Hill over again, when I run up to an officer with gold lace on his coat and lemon pie on his whiskers, and told him an old crazy Yankee out on deck was going to murder a poor sea sick Englishman, and the officer rushed out and took dad by the coat collar and made him quit, and when he found what the quarrel was about, he told dad all the chairs were private property belonging to the passengers, and for him to keep out of them, and he apologized to the Englishman and they went into the saloon and settled it with high balls, and dad beat the Englishman by drinking two high balls to his one. Then dad set into a poker game, with ten cents ante, and no limit, and they played along for a while until dad got four jacks, and he bet five dollars, and a Frenchman raised him five thousand dollars, and dad laid down his hand and said the game was too rich for his blood, and when he reached in his vest pocket for money to pay for his poker chips he found that his roll was gone, and he said he would leave his watch for security until he could go to his state room and get some money, and then he found that his watch had been pinched, and the Englishman said he would be good for it, and dad came out in the cabin and wanted me to help him find the widow, cause he said when she laid her head on his shoulder, to recover from her sickness, he felt a fumbling around his vest, but he thought it was nothing but his stomach wiggling to get ready for another engagement, but now he knew she had robbed him. Say, dad and I looked all over that boat for the widow, but she simply had evaporated. But land is in sight, and we shall land at Liverpool this afternoon, and dad is going to lay for the widow at the gang plank, and he won't do a thing to her. I guess not. Well, you will hear from me in London next, and I'll tell you if dad got his money and watch back.

   Hennery.

CHAPTER VII.

London, England.

Dear Old Man:

Well, sir, if a court sentenced me to live in this town, I would appeal the case, and ask the judge to temper his sentence with mercy, and hang me. Say, the fog here is so thick you have to feel around like a blind goddess, and when you show up through the fog you look about eighteen feet high, and you are so wet you want to be run through a clothes wringer every little while. For two days we never left the hotel, but looked out of the windows waiting for the fog to go by, and watching the people swim through it, without turning a hair. Dad was for going right to the Lord Mayor and lodging a complaint, and demanding that the fog be cleared off, so an American citizen could go about town and blow in his money, but I told him he could be arrested for treason. He come mighty near being arrested on the cars from Liverpool to London. When we got off the steamer and tried to find the widow who robbed dad of his watch and roll of money, but never found her, we were about the last passengers to reach the train, and when we got ready to get on we found these English cars that open on the sides, and they put you into a box stall with some other live stock, and lock you in, and once in a while a guard opens the door to see if you are dead from suffocation, or have been murdered by the other passengers. Dad kicked on going in one of the kennels the first thing, and said he wanted a parlor car; but the guard took dad by the pants and gave him a shove, and tossed me in on top of dad, and two other passengers and a woman in the compartment snickered, and dad wanted to fight all of 'em except the woman, but he concluded to mash her. When the door closed dad told the guard he would walk on his neck when the door opened, and that he was not an entry in a dog show, and he wanted a kennel all to himself, and asked for dog biscuit. Gee, but that guard was mad, and he gave dad a look that started the train going. I whispered to dad to get out his revolver, because the other passengers looked like hold up men, and he took his revolver out of his satchel and put it in his pistol pocket, and looked fierce, and the woman began to act faint, while the passengers seemed to be preparing to jump on dad if he got violent. When the train stopped at the first station I got out and told the guard that the old gentleman in there was from Helena, Montana, and that he had a reputation from St. Paul to Portland, and then I held up both hands the way train robbers make passengers hold up their hands. When I went back in the car dad was talking to the woman about her resembling a woman he used to know in the states, and he was just going to ask her how long she had been so beautiful, when the guard came to the side door and called the woman out into another stall, and then one of the passengers pulled out a pair of handcuffs and told dad he might as well surrender, because he was a Scotland yard detective and had spotted dad as an American embezzler, and if he drew that gun he had in his pocket there would be a dead Yankee in about four minutes. Well, I thought dad had nerve before, but he beat the band, right there. He unbuttoned his overcoat and put his finger on a Grand Army button in his buttonhole, and said, "Gentlemen, I am an American citizen, visiting the crowned heads of the old world, with credentials from the President of the United States, and day after tomorrow I have a date to meet your king, on official business that means much to the future peace of our respective countries. Lay a hand on me and you hang from the yard arm of an American battleship." Well, sir, I have seen a good many bluffs in my time, but I never saw the equal of that, for the detective turned white, and apologized, and asked dad and I out to luncheon at the next station, and we went and ate all there was, and when the time was up the detective disappeared and dad had to pay for the luncheon, but he kicked all the way to London, and the guard would not listen to his complaints, but told him if he tried to hold up the train he would be thrown out the window and run over by the train. We had the compartment to ourselves the rest of the way to London, except about an hour, when the guard shoved in a farmer who smelled like cows, and dad tried to get in a quarrel with him, about English roast beef coming from America, but the man didn't have his arguing clothes on, so dad began to find fault with me, and the man told dad to let up on the kid or he would punch his bloody 'ed off. That settled it, when the man dropped his "h," dad thought he was one of the nobility, and he got quite chummy with the Englishman, and then we got to London, and dad had a quarrel about his baggage, and after threatening to have a lot of fights he got his trunk on the roof of a cab, and in about an hour we got to the hotel, and then the fog began an engagement. If the fog here ever froze stiff, the town would look like a piece of ice with fish frozen in. Gee, but I would like to have it freeze in front of our hotel, so I could take an ax and go out and chop a frozen girl out, and thaw her till she came to.

 Say, old man, if anybody ever wants to treat you to a trip to Europe, don't come here, but go to some place where they don't think they can speak English. You can understand a Nitalian or a Frenchman, or a Dutchman, who can't speak English, and knows he can't, better than you can an Englishman who thinks he can speak English, and can't, "don't you know." Everything is "don't you know." If a servant gives you an evening paper, he says, "'Ere's your paiper, don't you know," and if a man should—I don't say they would, but if a man should give you a civil answer, when you asked him the name of a street, he would look at you as though you were a cannibal, and say, "Regent street, don't you know," and then he would act as though you had broken him of his rest. Dad asked more than a dozen men where Bill Astor lived, and of all the population of London I don't believe anybody knows, except one newsboy. We rode half a day on top of a bus, through streets so crowded that the horses had to creep, and dad hung on for fear the bus would be tipped over, and finally we got out into the suburbs, where the rich people live, and dad said we were right on the trail of King Edward, and we got off and loitered around, and dad saw a beautiful place, with a big iron fence, and a gate as big as a railroad bridge, and dad asked a newsboy who lived there, and the boy made up a face at dad and said, "H'astor, you bloke," and he put out his hand for a tip. It was the first civil answer dad had received in London, so he gave the boy a dollar. The boy fell over on the sidewalk, dead, and dad started to go away for fear he would be arrested for murder, but I kicked the boy on the pants, and he got up and yelled some kind of murdered English, and more than a dozen newsboys came on a gallop, and when the boy told them what had happened they all wanted dad to ask them questions. I told the boys dad was Andrew Carnegie, and that he was giving away millions of dollars, so when dad got to the gate of the beautiful H'astor place, the boys yelled Andrew Carnegie, and a flunkey flunked the gate open and dad and I went in, and walked up to the house. Astor was on the veranda, smoking a Missouri corn cob pipe, and drinking American beer, and seemed to be wishing he was back home in America. Dad marched right up to the veranda, like a veteran soldier, and Astor could see dad was an American by the dandruff on his coat collar, and Astor said, "You are an American citizen and you are welcome. Once I was like you, and didn't care a continental dam for anybody, but in a moment of passion I renounced my country, swore allegiance to this blawsted country, and everybody hates me here, and I don't dare go home to collect my rent for fear I will be quarantined at Ellis Island and sent back to England as an undesirable emigrant who has committed a crime, and is not welcome in the land where I was born. Old man, have a glass of Milwaukee beer and let's talk of your home and my birthplace, and forget that there is such a country as England." Dad sat down on the porch, and I went out on the lawn chasing peacocks and treeing guinea hens, and setting dogs on the swans, until a butler or a duke or something took me by the collar and shook me till my teeth got loose, and he took me back to the veranda and sat me down on the bottom step so hard my hair raised right up stiff, like a porcupine. Then I listened to dad and Astor talk about America, and I never saw a man who seemed to be so ashamed that he was a brevet Englishman, as he did. He said he had so much money that it made his headache to hear the interest accumulate, nights, when he couldn't sleep, and yet he had no more enjoyment than Dreyfus did on Devil's Island. He had automobiles that would fill our exposition building, horses and carriages by the score, but he never enjoyed a ride about London, because only one person in ten thousand knew him, and those who did looked upon him with pity and contempt because he had renounced his country to get solid with the English aristocracy, and nobody would speak to him unless they wanted to borrow money, and if they did borrow money from him he was afraid they would pay it back, and make him trouble counting it. He told dad he wanted to get back into America, and become a citizen again of that grand old country of the stars and stripes, and asked dad how he could do it, for he said he had rather work in a slaughter house in America than be a grand duke in England. I never saw dad look so sorry for a man as he did for Astor, and he told him the only way was to sell out his ranch in London and go back on an emigrant ship, take out his first papers, vote the democratic ticket and eventually become a citizen. Astor was thinking over the proposition, and dad had asked him if he was not afraid of dynamiters, when he shuddered and said every day he expected to be blown sky high, and finally he smelled something burning and said the smell reminded him of an American 4th of July. You see, I had been sitting still on the step of the veranda so long I got nervous, for something exciting, so I took a giant firecracker out of my pocket and lit the long tail, and shoved it under the porch and looked innocent, and just then one of the flunkies with the tightest pants you ever saw came along and patted me on the head and said I was a nice boy, and that made me mad, and when he went to sit down beside me on the step I took my horse chestnut out of my pocket and put it on the step just where he sat down, and how it happened to come out so I don't know, it must have been Providence.

Now I Lay Me Down to Sleep 094

You see just as the flunkey flunked on the chestnut burr, the fire cracker went off, and the man jumped up and said "'Ells-fire, h'am blowed," and he had his hands on his pants, and the air was full of smoke, and dad got on his knees and said, "Now I lay me," and Mr. Astor fainted all over a rocking chair and tipped beer bottles on the veranda and more than forty servants came, and I told dad to come on, and we got outside the gate, ahead of the police, and got a cab and drove quicker than scat to the hotel, and I ast dad what he thought it was that went off, and he said "You can search me," but he said he had got enough of trying to reform escaped Americans, and we got in the hotel and laid low, and the newspapers told about a dynamite outrage, and laid it to anarchists. Well I must close, cause we are going to see the American minister and get a date to meet King' Edward. We won't do a thing to Edward.

Yours,
Hennery.

CHAPTER VIII.

London, England.—My Dear Chum: I received your letter yesterday, and it made me homesick. Gee, but if I could be home there with you and go down to the swimming hole and get in all over, and play tag in the sand, and tie some boy's pants and shirt in knots, and yell that the police are coming, and all grab our clothes under our arms and run across lots with no clothes on, and get in a barn and put on our clothes, and dry our hair by pounding it with a stick, so we would not get licked when we got home, life would be worth living, but here all I do is to dodge people on the streets and see them look cross when they step on me.

Say, boy, you will never know your luck in being a citizen of good old America, instead of a subject of Great Britain, because you have got to be rich or be hungry here, and if you are too rich you have got no appetite. You have heard of the roast beef of old England, but nobody eats it but the dukes and bankers. The working men never even saw a picture of a roast beef, and yet we look upon all Englishmen as beef-eaters, but three-fourths of the people in this town look hungry and discouraged, and they never seem to know whether they are going to have any supper.

I went down to a market this morning where the middle class and the very poor people buy their supplies, and it would make you sick to see them. They buy small loaves of bread and a penny's worth of tea, and that is breakfast, and if a man is working he takes some of the bread to work for lunch, and the wife or mother buys a carrot or a quarter of a cabbage, and maybe a bone with a piece of meat about as big as a fish bait, and that makes supper, with a growler of beer.

Say, the chunk of meat with a bone that an American butcher would throw at a dog that he had never been introduced to would be a banquet for a large family over here.

I have been down into the White Chapel district, which is the Five Points of London, and of the thousands of tough people I saw there was not a man but looked as though he would cut your liver out for a shilling, and every woman was drunk on gin. What there is about gin that makes it the national beverage for bad people beats me, for it looks like water, tastes like medicine and smells like cold storage eggs. At home when a person takes a drink of beer or whisky he at least looks happy for a minute, and maybe he laughs, but here nobody laughs unless somebody gets hurt, and that seems to tickle everybody in the White Chapel district.

The people look mad and savage when they are not drinking, as though they were only looking for an opportunity to commit murder, and then when they take a drink of gin, instead of smiling and smacking their lips as though it was good and braced them up, they look as though they had been stabbed with a dirk and they put on a look of revenge, as though they would like to wring a child's neck or cut holes in the people they meet.

Two drinks of gin makes a man or woman look as though they had swallowed a buzz saw. I always thought drinking liquor made people think they were enjoying themselves, or that they took it to drive away care and make them forget their sorrows, but when these people drink gin they seem to do it the way an American drinks carbolic acid, to end the whole business quick.

At home the drinker drinks to make him feel like he was at a picnic. Here every drinker acts like a suicide, who only hopes that he may commit a murder before the gin ends his career. And there are hundreds of thousands of people in this town who have no ambition except to get a bit of bread to sustain them till they can get a drink of gin, and gradually they let up on bread entirely and feed on gin, and look like mad dogs and snarl at everybody they see, as much as to say: "What are you going to do about it?"

Snarl at Everybody They See 101

A good square American meal would give them a fit, and they would go to a hospital and die if the meal could not be got out of them.

Gosh, but I was glad to get out of the White Chapel district, and I kept looking back for fear one of the men or women would slit me up the back with a butcher knife, and laugh like an insane asylum inmate.

Do you know, those people who drink gin and go hungry are different from our American murderers. Our murderers will assault you with a smile, rob you with a joke on their tongue's end, and give you back car fare when they hold you up, and if they murder you they will do it easy and lay you out with your hands across on your breast and notify the coroner, but your White Chapel murderer wants to disembowel you and cut you up into chunks, and throw your remains head first into something nasty, and if you have money enough on your person to buy a bottle of gin your murderer is as well satisfied as though he got a roll. Some men in our country commit murders in order to get money to lay away so they can live a nice, respectable life and be good ever afterwards, but your slum murderer in London just kills because his stomach craves a drink, and when he gets it he is tame, like a tiger that has eaten a native of India.

You may think this letter is a solemn occasion because I tell you about things that are not funny, but if you ever traveled abroad you will find that there is no fun anywhere except in America unless you make it or buy it.

We are taking in the solemn things first in order to get dad's mind in a condition so he can be cured of things he thinks ail him. I took dad to the Tower of London, and when we got out of it he wanted to have America interfere and have the confounded place burned down and grass sown on the site and a park made of it.

The tower covers 13 acres of ground, and there are more things brought to a visitor's attention that ought to be forgotten than you ever thought about.

I remember attending the theater at home and seeing Richard the Third played, and I remember how my sympathies were aroused for the two little boy princes that were murdered by Richard the Third, but I thought it was a fake play, and that there was nothing true about it, but, by gosh, it was right here in the Tower of London that the old hump-backed cuss murdered those little princes, and dad and I stood right on the spot, and the beef-eater who showed us around told us all the particulars. Dad was indignant, and said to the beef-eater:

Stood Around and Let Richard Kill Those Princes 098

"Do you mean to tell me you stood around and let Richard kill those princes without uttering a protest or protecting them or ringing for the police? By the great hornspoon, you must have been accessory to the fact, and you ought to be arrested and hung," and dad pounded his cane on the stone floor and looked savage.

The beef-eater got red in the face and said: "Begging your pardon, don't you know, but h'l was not 'ere at the time. This 'istory was made six 'undred years ago."

Dad begged the man's pardon and told him he supposed the boys were murdered a year or two ago, and he gave the beef-eater a dollar, and he was so gratified I think he would have had a murder committed for dad right there and then if dad had insisted on it.

You feel in going through the tower like you was in an American slaughter house, for it was here that kings and queens were beheaded by the dozen. They showed us axes that were used to behead people, and blocks that the heads of the victims were laid on, and the places where the heads fell on the floor. It seemed that in olden times when a king or a queen got too gay, the anti-kings or queens would go to the palace and catch the king or queen in the act, and take them by the neck and hustle them to the tower, and when a king or queen got in the tower they went out on the installment plan, and after being thrown in the gutter for the mob to recognize, and walk on the bodies, they would bring them back in the tower, and seal them up in a pigeon hole for future generations to cry over.

All my life I have had in our house to look at a picture of beautiful Anne Boleyn, and here I stood right where her head was cut off, and I couldn't help thinking of how we in America got our civilization from the descendants of the English people who cut her head off.

By ginger, old chum, it made me hot. I didn't care to look at the old armor, or the crown jewels, which make you think of a cut glass factory, but I reveled in the scenes of the beheading. I never was stuck much on kings and queens, but it seems to me if they had to murder them they ought to have given 'em a show, and let them fight for their lives, instead of getting into a trap, like you would entice a rat with cheese, and then cut their heads off.

I suppose it is right here that we inherited the desire to lynch and burn at the stake the negroes that commit crime and won't confess at home. When anything is born in the blood you can't get rid of it without taking a dose of patriotism and purifying the blood, and I advise you never to visit the Tower of London, unless you want to feel like going out and killing some one that is tied up with a rope.

Hearing of these murders and seeing the place where they were committed does not give you an idea of fair play and you don't feel like taking some one of your size when you fight, but you get to thinking that if you could catch a cripple who couldn't defend himself you would like to take a baseball club and maul the stuffing out of him. You become imbued with the idea that if you went to war you would not want to stand up and fight fair, but that you would like to get your enemy in a bunch and drop dynamite down on him from a balloon, and kill all in sight, and sail away with an insane laugh.

Gee, but another day in this tower, and I would want to go home and murder ma, or the neighbors.

The only thing we have got in America that compares with the Tower of London and its associates is the Leutgert sausage factory in Chicago, where Leutgert got his wife into the factory, murdered her, and is alleged to have cut her up in pieces and made sausage of the meat, given the pieces with gristle in to his dogs, boiled the bones until they would run into the sewer, dissolved the remnants in concentrated lye, and sold the sausage to the lumber Jacks in the pine woods.

I expect Chicago will buy that sausage factory and make a show of it, as London does the tower, and you can go and see it, and feel that you are as full of modern history as I am of ancient history, here in London.

I could see that dad was getting nervous every time a new beheading was described to us, and I thought it was time to wake him up. In going through the room where the old armor was displayed the beef eater told us who wore the different pieces of armor, and he said at times the spirit of the dead came back to the tower and occupied the armor, and I noticed that dad shied at some of the pieces of armor, so when we got right into the midst of it, and there was armor on every side, and dad and the beef eater were ahead of me, and dad was walking fast in order to get out quick, I pushed over one of the pieces, and it went crashing to the floor and the noise was like a boiler factory exploding, and the dust of centuries rose up, and the noise echoed down the halls.

Well, you'd a died to see dad and the beef eater. Dad turned pale and got down on his knees, and I think he began to pray, if he knows how, and he trembled like a leaf, and the beef eater got behind a set of armor that Cromwell or some old duck used to wear, and said, "Wot in the bloody 'ell is the matter with the h'armor?" and then a lot of other beef eaters came, and they thought dad was the spirit of King John, and they stampeded, and finally I got dad to stop praying, or whatever it was that he was doing, and I led him out, and when he got into the open air he recovered and said. "'Ennery, 'hi have got to get out of Lunnon, don't you know, because me 'eart is palpitating," and we went back to the 'otel, to see if our invitation to visit King Hedward had arrived.

Say, we are getting so we talk just like English coachmen, and you won't hundredstand us when we get 'ome. Yours, with a haccent.

'Ennery.

CHAPTER IX.

London, H-england.—Dear Uncle Ezra: The worst is over, and dad and I have both touched a king. Not the way you think, touching a king for a hand-out, or borrowing his loose change, the way you used to touch dad when you had to pay for your goods, but just taking hold of his hand and shaking it in good old United States fashion.

The American minister arranged it for us. He told somebody that Peck's Bad Boy and his dad were in town, and just wanted to size up a king and see how he averaged up with United States politicians, and the king set an hour for us to call.

Well, you'd a dide to see dad fix up. Everybody said, when we showed our card at the hotel, notifying us that we were expected at Marlboro House at such a time, that we would be expected to put on plenty of dog. That is what an American from Kalamazoo, who sells breakfast food, said, and the hotel people said we would be obliged to wear knee breeches and dancing pumps and silk socks, and all that kind of rot, and men's furnishers began to call upon us to take our measure for clothes, but when they told us how much it would cost, dad kicked. He said he had a golf suit he had made in Oshkosh at the time of the tournament, that every one in Oshkosh said was out of sight, and was good enough for any king, and so he rigged up in it, and I hired a suit at a masquerade place, and dad hired a coat, kind of red, to go with his golf pants and socks, and he wore canvas tennis shoes.

Suit he Had Made in Oshkosh 111

I looked like a picture out of a fourteenth century book, but dad looked like a clown in a circus. One of dad's calves made him look as though he had a milk leg, cause the padding would not stay around where the calf ought to be, but worked around towards his shin. We went to Marlboro House in a hansom cab, and all the way there the driver kept looking down from the hurricane deck, through the scuttle hole, to see if we were there yet, and he must have talked with other cab drivers in sign language about us, for every driver kept along with us, looked at us and laughed, as though we were a wild west show.

On the way to the king's residence it was all I could do to keep dad braced up to go through the ordeal. He was brave enough before we got the invitation, and told what he was going to say to the king, and you would think he wasn't afraid of anybody, but when we got nearer to the house and dad thought of going up to the throne and seeing a king in all his glory, surrounded by his hundreds of lords and dukes and things, a crown on his head, and an ermine cloak trimmed with red velvet, and a six-quart milk pan full of diamonds, some of them as big as a chunk of alum, dad weakened, and wanted to give the whole thing up and go to a matinee, but I wouldn't have it, and told him if he didn't get into the king row now that I would shake him right there in London and start in business as a Claude Duval highwayman and hold up stage coaches, and be hung on Tyburn Tree, as I used to read about in my history of Sixteen-String Jack and other English highwaymen. Dad didn't want to see the family disgraced, so he let the cabman drive on, but he said if we got out of this visit to royalty alive, it was the last tommyrot he would indulge in.

Well, old man, it is like having an operation for appendicitis, you feel better when you come out from under the influence of the chloroform and the doctor shows you what they took out of you, and you feel that you are going to live, unless you grow another vermiform appendix. We were driven into a sort of Central park, and up to a building that was big as a lot of exposition buildings, and the servants took us in charge and walked us through long rooms covered with pictures as big as side show pictures at a circus, but instead of snake charmers and snakes and wild men of Borneo and sword swallowers, the king's pictures were about war, and women without much clothes on from the belt up. Gosh, but some of those pictures made you think you could hear the roar of battle and smell gun powder, and dad acted as though he wanted to git right down on the marble floor and dig a rifle pit big enough to git into.

They walked us around like they do when you are being initiated into a secret society, only they didn't sing, "Here comes the Lobster," and hit you with a dried bladder. The servants that were conducting us laffed. I had never seen an Englishman laff before, and it was the most interesting thing I saw in London. Most Englishmen look sorry about something, as though some dear friend died every day, and their faces seem to have grown that way. So when they laff it seems as though the wrinkles would stay there, unless they treated their faces with massage. They were laughing at dad's dislocated calf, and his scared appearance, as though he was going to receive the thirty-second degree, and didn't know whether they were going to throw him over a precipice or pull him up to the roof by the hind legs. We passed a big hall clock, and it struck just when we were near it, and of all the "Hark, from the tombs" sounds I ever heard, that clock took the cake. Dad thought it sounded like a death knell, and he would have welcomed the turning in of a fire alarm as a sound that meant life everlasting, beside that doleful sound.

After we had marched about three mile heats, and passed the chairs of the noble grand and the senior warden, and the exalted ruler, we came to a bronze door as big as the gate to a cemetery, and the grand conductor gave us a few instructions about how to back out fifteen feet from the presence of the king, when we were dismissed, and then he turned us over to a little man who was a grand chambermaid, I understood the fellow to say. The door opened, and we went in, and dad's misplaced calf was wobbling as though he had locomotor attacks-ye.

Well, there were a dozen or so fellows standing around, and they all had on some kind of uniforms, with gold badges on their breasts, and in the midst of them was a little, sawed-off fat fellow, not taller than five feet six, but a perfect picture of the cigar advertisements of America for a cigar named after the king. I expected to see a king as big as Long John Wentworth of Chicago, a great big fellow that could take a small man by the collar and throw him over a house, and I felt hurt at the small size of the king of Great Britain, but, gosh, he is just like a Yankee, when you get the formality shook off.

We bowed and dad made a courtesy like an old woman, and the king came forward with a smile that ought to be imitated by every Englishman. They all imitate his clothes and his hats and his shoes, but he seems to be the only Englishman that smiles. Maybe it is patented, and nobody has a right to smile without paying a royalty, but the good-natured smile of King Edward is worth more than stomach bitters, and the English ought to be allowed to copy it. There is no more solemn thing than a party of Englishmen together in America, unless it is a party of speculators that are short on wheat, or a gathering of defeated politicians when the election returns come in. But the king is as jolly as though he had not a note coming due at the bank, and you would think he was a good, common citizen, after working hours, at a round beer table, with two schooner loads in the hold and another schooner on the way, frothing over the top of the stein. That is the feeling I had for the king when he came up to us and greeted dad as the father of the bad boy and patted me on the shoulder and said: "And so you are the boy that has made more trouble than any boy in the world, and had more fun than anybody, and made them all stand around and wonder what was coming next. You're a wonder. Strange the American people never thought of killing you." I said yessir, and tried to look innocent, and then the king told dad to sit down, and for me to come and stand by his knee, and by ginger, when he patted me on the cheek, and his soft hand squeezed my hand, and he looked into my eyes with the most winning expression, I did not wonder that all the women were in love with him, and that all Englishmen would die for him.

He asked dad all about America, its institutions, the president, and everything, and dad was just so flustered that he couldn't say much, until the king said something about the war between the States, in which the southern states achieved a victory. I don't know whether the king said that just to wake dad up, 'cause dad had a grand army button on his coat, but dad choked up a little, and then began to explode, a little at a time, like a bunch of firecrackers, and finally he went off all in a bunch. Dad said: "Look a here, Mr. King, some one has got you all balled up about that war. I know, because I was in it, and now the north and the south are United, and can whip any country that wants to fight a champion, and will go out and get a reputation, by gosh!"

The king laughed at touching dad off, and asked dad what was the matter of America and Great Britain getting together and making all nations know when they had better keep their places, and quit talking about fighting. Dad said he never would consent to America and Great Britain getting together to fight any country until Ireland got justice and was ready to come into camp on an equality, and the king said he would answer for the Irishmen of Ireland if dad would pledge the Irishmen of America, 'cause we had about as many Irishmen in America as he had in Ireland, and dad said if the king would give Ireland what she asked for, he would see that the Irishmen in America would sing God Save the King.

I guess dad and the king would have settled the Irish question in about fifteen minutes, and signed a treaty, only a servant brought in a two-quart bottle of champagne, and dad and the king hadn't drank a quart apiece before dad started to sing "My Country Tis of Thee, Sweet Land of Libertee," and the king sang "God Save the King," and, by thunder, it was the same tune, and tears came into dad's eyes, and the king took out his handkerchief and wiped his nose, and I bellered right out, and the king rose and offered a toast to America and everybody in it, and they swallered it, and dad said there was enough juice left in the bottle for one more round, and he proposed a toast to all the people of Great Britain, including the Irish and the king who loved them, and down she went, and they were standing up. And I told dad it was time to go.

Say, it was great, Uncle Ezra, and I wish you could have been there, and there had been another bottle. The only thing that happened to mar the reunion of dad and the king was when we were going out backwards, bowing. There was a little hassock back of me, and I kicked it back of dad, and when dad's heels struck it he went over backwards and struck on his golf pants, and dad said: "El, 'Ennery, I'ave broken my bloomink back, but who cares," and when the servants picked dad up and took him out in the hall and marched us to the entrance, dad got in the cab, gave the grand hailing sign of distress, started to sing God save something or other, and went to sleep in the cab, and I took him to the hotel.

Yours,
Hennery.

CHAPTER X.

London, England.—My Dear Old Skate: Well, if we are going to see any of the other countries on this side of the water before our return ticket expires, we have got to be getting a move on, and dad says in about a week we will be doing stunts in Paris that will bring about a revolution, and wind up the republic of France, and seat some nine-spot on the throne that Napoleon used to wear out his buckskin pants on.

Dad asked me tother day what I cared most to see in London, and I told him I wanted to visit Newgate prison, and the places made famous by the bold highwaymen of a century or two ago. He thought I was daffy, but when I told him how I had read "Claude Duval" and "Six-teen-String Jack" and all the highway literature, in the haymow, when dad thought I was weeding the garden, he confessed that he used to hunt those yellow covered books out of the manger when I was not reading them, and that he had read them all himself, when I thought he was studying for his campaign speeches, and so he said he would go with me. So we visited Homestead Heath, where Claude Duval used to ride "Black Bess," and hold up people who traveled at night in post chaises, and we found splendid spots where there had been more highway robbery going on than any place east of Missouri, but I was disgusted when I thought what chumps those old highway robbers were, compared to the American highway robbers and hold up men of the present day.

In Claude Duval's time he had a brace of flintlock pistols, which he had to examine the priming every time a victim showed up, and while he was polite when he robbed a duchess, he used to kill people all right, though if they had had cameras at that time the flash from the priming pan would have taken a flash-light picture of the robber, so he could have been identified when he rode off in the night to a roadside inn and filled up on beer, while he counted the ten shillings he had taken from the silk purse of the victim. Why, one of our American gangs that hold up a train, and get an express safe full of greenbacks, and shoots up a mess of railroad hands and passengers with Winchesters and automatic pistols, and blows up cars with dynamite and gets away and has to have a bookkeeper and a cashier to keep their bank accounts straight, could give those old Claude Duvals and Sixteen-String Jacks cards and spades.

But civilization, dad says, has done much for the highway robbery business, and he says we in America have arrived at absolute perfection. However, I was much interested in looking over the ground where my first heroes lived and died, and did business, and when we went to the prisons where they were confined, and were shown where Tyburn Tree stood, that so many of them were hung on, tears came to my eyes at the thought that I was on the sacred ground where my heroes croaked, and went to their deaths with smiles on their faces, and polite to the last. The guard who showed us around thought that dad and I were relatives of the deceased highwaymen, and when we went away he said to dad: "Call again, Mr. Duval. Always glad to serve any of the descendants of the heroes. What line of robbery are you in, Mr. Duval?" Dad was mad, but he told the guard he was now on the stock exchange, and so we maintained the reputation of the family.

Then we hired horses and took a horse back ride through Rotten Row, where everybody in London that has the price, rides a horse, and no carriages are allowed. Dad was an old cavalry man forty years ago, and he is stuck on his shape when he is on a horse, but he came near breaking up the horse back parade the day we went for the ride. The liveryman gave us two bob-tailed nags, a big one for dad and a small one for me, but they didn't have any army saddle for dad, and he had to ride on one of these little English saddles, such as jockeys ride races on, and dad is so big where he sits on a saddle that you couldn't see the saddle, and I guess they gave dad a hurdle jumper, because when we got right amongst the riders, men and women, his horse began to act up, and some one yelled, "Tally-ho," and that is something about fox hunting, not a coach, and the horse jumped a fence and dad rolled off over the bowsprit and went into a ditch of dirty water.

Dad Rolled off over the Bowsprit 128

The horse went off across a field, and the policeman fished dad out of the ditch, and run him through a clothes wringer or something, and got him dried out, and sent him to the hotel in an express wagon, and I rode my horse back to the liveryman and told him what happened to dad, and they locked me up in a box stall until somebody found the horse, 'cause they thought dad was a horse thief, and they held me for ransom. But dad came around before night and paid my ransom, and we were released. Dad says Rotten Row is rotten, all right enough, and by ginger it is, 'cause he has not got the smell of that ditch off his clothes yet.

Now he has got a new idea, and that is to go to some country where there are bandits, different from the bandits here in London, and be captured and taken to the mountain fastnesses, and held for ransom until our government makes a fuss about it, and sends warships after-us. I tell dad it would be just our luck to have our government fail to try to get us, and the bandits might cut our heads off and stick them on a pole as a warning to people not to travel unless they had a ransom concealed about their clothes. But dad says he is out to see all the sights, and he is going to be ransomed before he gets home, if it takes every dollar our government has got. I think he is going to work the bandit racket when we get to Turkey, but, by ginger, he can leave me at a convent, because I don't want one of those crooked sabers run into me and turned around like a corkscrew. Dad says I can stay in a harem while he goes to the mountains with the bandits, and I don't know as I care, as they say a harem is the most interesting place in Turkey. You know the pictures we have studied in the old grocery, where a whole bunch of beautiful women are practicing using soap in a marble bath.

Well, don't you say anything to ma about it, but dad has got his foot in it clear up to the top button. It isn't anything scandalous, though there is a woman at the bottom of it. You see, we used to know a girl that left home to go out into the world and earn her own living. She elocuted some at private parties and sanitariums, to entertain people that were daffy, and were on the verge of getting permanent bats in their belfry, and after a few years she got on the stage, and made a bunch of money, and went abroad. And then she had married a titled person, and everybody supposed she was a duchess, or a countess, and ma wanted us to inquire about her when we got over here. Ma didn't want us to go and hunt her up to board with her, or anything, but just to get a glimpse of high life, and see if our poor little friend was doing herself proud in her new station in life.

Isn't Money Enough in the Whole Family to Wad a Gun

Gee, but dad found her, and she ain't any more of a duchess than I am. Her husband is a younger son of a titled person, but there isn't money enough in the whole family to wad a gun, and our poor girl is working in a shop, or store, selling corsets to support a lazy, drunken husband and a whole mess of children, and while she is seven removes from a duchess, she does not rank with the woman who washes her mother's clothes at home. Gosh, but dad was hot when he found her, and after she told him about her situation in life he gave her a yellow-backed fifty-dollar bill, and came back to the hotel mad, and wanted to pack up and go somewhere else, where he didn't know any titled-persons.

That night a couple of dukes came around to the hotel to sell dad some stock in a diamond mine in South Africa, and they got to talking about how English society held over our crude American society, until dad got an addition to the mad he had when he called on our girl, and when one of the dukes said America was being helped socially by the marriage of American women to titled persons, dad got a hot box, like a stalled freight train.

Says dad, says he: "You Johnnies are a lot of confidence men, who live only to rope in rich American girls, so you can marry them and have their dads lift the mortgages on your ancestral estates, and put on tin roofs in place of the mortgages, 'cause a mortgage will not shed rain, and you get their money and spend it on other women." One of the dukes turned red like a lobster, and I think he is a lobster, anyway, and he was going to make dad stop talking, but the duke didn't know dad, and he continued. Says dad, says he: "I know a rich old man in the States, who made ten million dollars on pickles, or breakfast food, and he had a daughter that was so homely they couldn't keep a clock going in the house.

"She came over here and got exposed to a duke, and she had never been vaccinated, and the first her father knew she caught the duke, and came; home, and he followed her. Say, he didn't know enough to pound sand, and the old man got several doctors for her, but they couldn't break up the duke fever, and finally the old pickle citizen asked him how much the mortgage was, and how much they could live on, and he bought her the duke, and sent them off, and the duke covered his castle with building paper, so it would hold water, and they set up housekeeping with a hundred servants. Then the duke wanted a racing stable, after the baby came, and the old pickle man went over to see the baby, and it looked so much like the old man that he invested in a racing stable, and the servants bowed low to the old man and called him 'Your 'ighness,' and that settled the old pickle person, and he fell into the trap of building a townhouse in London.

"Then he went home and made some more pickles, and the daughter cabled him to come right over, as they had been invited to entertain the king and a lot of other face cards in the pack. And the old man thought it would be great to get in the king row himself, so he shoveled a lot of big bills into some packing trunks and went over to fix up for the king. The castle had to be redecorated for about six miles, up one corridor and down the other, but Old Pickles stood the raise, because he thought it would be worth the money to be on terms of intimacy with a king.

"Then when it was all ready, and the old man was going to stand at the front door and welcome the king, they made him go to his room, back about a half a mile in the rear of the castle, and for two weeks old Pickles had his meals brought to his room, and when it was over, and his sentence had expired, he was let out, and all he saw of the grand entertainment to the crowned heads was a ravine full of empty wine bottles, a case of jimjams for a son-in-law, a case of nervous prostration for a daughter, and hydrophobia for himself. My old pickle friend has got, at this date, three million good pickle dollars invested in your d—d island, and all he has to show for it is a sick daughter, neglected by a featherhead of a husband, who will only speak to old pickles when he wants more money, and a grandchild that may die teething at any time. You are a nice lot of ducks to talk to me about your English society being better than our American civilization. You get," and dad drove the dukes out.

I think they are going to have dad arrested for treason. But don't tell ma, 'cause she may think treason serious.

Yours,

Hennery.

CHAPTER XI.

Paris, France.—My Dear Uncle Ezra: Dad is in an awful state here, and I do not know what to do with him. We struck this town all in a heap, and the people seemed to be paralyzed so they couldn't speak, except to make motions and make noises that we could not interpret. This is the first time dad and I have been in a place where nobody understood our language. Ordinarily we would take pleasure in teaching people to speak the English language, but in coming across the English channel dad and I both got something we never got on the water before. Ordinary seasickness is only an incident, that makes you wish you were dead—just temporary, but when it wears off you can enjoy your religion and victuals as well as ever, but the seasickness that the English channel gives you is a permanent investment, like government bonds that you cut coupons off of. I 'spect we shall be sick always now, and worse every other day, like chills and fever.

Say, a boat on the English channel does not roll, or pitch, at intervals, like a boat on ordinary water, but it does stunts like a broncho that has been poisoned by eating loco-weeds, and goes into the air and dives down under, and shakes itself like a black bass with a hook in its mouth, and rolls over like a trained dog, and sits up on its hind legs and begs, and then walks on its fore paws, and seems to jump through hoops, and dig for woodchucks, and all the time the water boils like 'pollinarius, full of bubbles, and it gives you the hiccups to look at it, and it flows every way at the same time, and the wind comes from the fourteen quarters at once, and blows hot if you are too hot and want a cool breeze, and if you are too cold, and want a warm breeze to keep you alive, it comes right from the north pole, and you just perish in your tracks.

Gee, but it is awful. When you get seasick on an ordinary ocean, you know where to locate the disease, and you know where to go for relief, and when you have got relieved you know that you are alive, but an English channel seasickness is as different from any other as an alcohol jag is different from a champagne drunk. This English channel seasickness begins on your toes, and you feel as though the toenails were being pulled out with pincers, and the veins in your legs seem to explode, your arms wilt like lettuce in front of a cheap grocery, your head seems to be struck with a pile-driver and telescoped down into your spine, and your stomach feels as though you had swallowed a telephone pole with all of the cross arms and wires and glass insulators, and you wish lightning would strike you. Gosh, but dad was hot when he found that he was sick that way, and when we got ashore he wanted to kill the first man he met.

He thinks that it is a crime for a man not to understand the English language, and when he tells what he wants, and the man he is talking to shrugs his shoulders and laughs, and brings him something else, he wants to pull his gun and begin to shoot up the town, and only for me he would have killed people before this, but now he takes it out in scowling at people who do not understand him. Dad seems to think that if he cannot make a man understand what he says, all he has to do is to swear at the man, but there is no universal language of profanity, so the more dad swears the more the nervous Frenchman smiles, and acts polite.

I think the French people are the politest folks I ever knew. If a Frenchman had to kick a person out of doors, he would wear a felt slipper, and after he had kicked you he would place his hand on his heart, and bow, and look so sorry, and hurt, that you would want to give him a tip.

O, but this tipping business is what is breaking dad's heart. I think if the servants would arrange a syndicate to rob dad of two or three dollars a day, by pocket picking, or sneak thieving, he would overlook it, and say that as long as it was one of the customs of the country we should have to submit to it, but when he has paid his bill, with everything charged extra, and the servants line up and look appealingly, or mad, as the case may be, dad is the hardest man to loosen that ever was, but if they seem to look the other way, and not, apparently, care whether they get a cent or not, dad would go and hunt them up, and divide his roll with them. Dad is not what you would call a "tight wad," if you let him shed his money normally, when he feels the loosening coming on, but you try to work him by bowing and cringing, and his American spirit gets the better of him, and he looks upon the servant as pretty low down. I have told him that the tipping habit is just as bad in America as in France, but he says in America the servant acts as though he never had such a thought as getting a tip, and when you give him a quarter or other tip he looks puzzled, as though he did not just recall what he had done to merit such treatment, but finally puts the money in his pocket with an air as though he would accept it in trust, to be given to some deserving person at the first opportunity, and then he smiles, and gets away, and blows in the tip for something wet and strong.

I told dad if he would just ignore the servants, as though he did not understand that they expected a tip, that he would be all right, so when we got ready to move from the hotel to private rooms dad never gave any servant a tip. Well, I don't know what the servants did to our baggage, but they must have marked it with a smallpox sign, or something, for nobody would touch it for several hours, but finally a baggage man took it and started for our apartments, and got lost and didn't show up for two days, and when it was finally landed on the sidewalk nobody would carry it upstairs, and dad and I had to lug it up two flights, and I thought dad would have apoplexy.

Coughs up a Tip Every Time 143

We found a guide who could talk New Orleans English and he said it would cost three dollars to square it with the servants at the hotel, and have the boycott removed from our baggage, and dad paid it, and now he coughs up a tip every time he sees a servant look at him. He pays when he goes in a restaurant and when he comes out, and says he is cured of trying to reform the customs of anybody else's country.

We have engaged a guide to stay with us day and night. The guide took us out for a bat last night, and dad had the time of his life. Dad has drank a good deal of spiritous and malt liquors in his time, but I don't think he ever indulged much in champagne at three or four dollars a bottle at home. Maybe he has been saving himself up till he got over here, where champagne is cheap and it takes several quarts to make you see angels. The guide took us to one of these bullyvards, where there are tables out on the sidewalk, and you can eat and drink and look at the dukes and counts and dutchesses and things promenading up and down, flirting like sin, and we sat down to a table and ordered things to eat and drink, and dad looked like Uncle Sam, and felt his oats.

A Tone of Voice That Meant Trouble 138

When he had drank a few thimblefuls of absinthe, and some champagne, and eat a plateful of frogs, he was just ripe for trouble. A woman and a man at an adjoining table had one of these white dogs that is sheared like a hedge fence, with spots of long hair left on in places, and dad coaxed the dog over to our table and began to feed him frogs' legs, and the woman began to talk French out loud, and look cross at dad, and the count that was with her came over to our table and looked at dad in a tone of voice that meant trouble, and said something sassy, and the guide said the man wanted to fight a duel because dad had contaminated the woman's dog, and dad got mad and offered to wipe out the whole place, and he got up with a champagne bottle and looked defiance at the count, and the waiters began to scatter, when the woman came up to dad and begged him not to hurt the count, and as she spoke broken English dad could understand her, and she looked so beautiful, and her eyes were filled with tears, and dad relented and said: "Don't cry, dear, I won't hurt the little runt." She was so glad dad was not going to kill the count that she threw herself into his arms and thanked dear America for producing such a grand citizen, such a brave man as dad, who could forego the pleasure of killing a poor, weak man who had insulted him, particularly as dad's wild Indian ancestry made it hard for him to refrain from blood.

I Won't Hurt the Little Runt 145

Well, dad's face was a study, as he braced up and held that 150 pounds of white meat in his arms, with all the people looking on, and he seemed proud and heroic, and he stroked her hair and told her not to worry, and finally she hied herself away from dad and the count took her away, and they went up the bullyvard, and after all was quiet again dad said: "Hennery, let this be a lesson to you. When you are tempted to commit a rash act and avenge an insult in blood, stop and think of the sorrow and shame that will come to you if you draw your gun too quick, and have a widow on your hands as the result. Suppose I had killed that shrimp, the face of his widow would have haunted me always, and I would have wanted to die. Don't ever kill anybody, my boy, if you can settle a dispute by shaking the dice."

Well, dad ordered some more wine, and as he drank it, he allowed the populace to admire him and say things about the great American millionaire, who spent money like water and was too brave to fight. Then dad called for his check to pay his bill, and when he felt in his pocket for his roll of bills, he hadn't a nickel and the woman, when she was in his arms, weeding with one hand, had gone through dad's pockets with the other. Dad felt for his watch, to see what time it was, and his watch was gone, and the waiter was waiting for the money and dad tried to explain that he had been buncoed, and the head waiter came and begun to act sassy, and then they called a policeman to stay by us till the money was produced, and everybody at the other tables laughed, and dad turned blue, and I thought he would have a fit. Finally, the guide began to talk, and the result was that a policeman went home with us, and dad found money enough to pay the bill, but he talked language that caused the landlady to ask us to find a new place.

Tried to Explain That he Had Been Buncoed 148

The next morning the guide showed up with an officer who had a warrant for dad for hugging a woman in a public cafe, and it seemed as though we were in for it, but the guide said he could settle the whole business by paying the officer $20, and dad paid it and I think the guide and the officer divided the money. Say, this is the greatest town we have struck yet for excitement, and I guess dad will not have a chance to think of his sickness.

This morning we went into a big department store, and, by gosh! we found the count that dad was going to fight was a floor-walker, and the countess was behind a counter selling soap. When dad saw the count leering at him, he put his hand on his pistol pocket and yelled a regular cowboy yell, and the count rushed down into the basement, the soap countess fainted, and the police took dad to the police station, and all day the guide and I have been trying to get him out on bail. If we get dad out of this we are going to put a muzzle on him. Well, if anyone asks you if I am having much of a time abroad, you can tell them the particulars.

P. S.—We got dad out for $20 and costs, and he says he will blow Paris up before night. We are going up to the top of the Eiffel tower this afternoon, to count our money, as dad dassent take out his pocketbook anywhere on the ground for fear of being robbed.

Yours full of frogs.

Hennery.

CHAPTER XII.

Paris, France.—Old Pardner in Crime: I got your letter, telling me about the political campaign that is raging at home, and when I read it to dad he wanted to go right out and fill up on campaign whisky and yell for his presidential candidate, but he couldn't find any whisky, so he has not tried to carry any precincts of Paris for our standard-bearer.

There is something queer about the liquor here. There is no regular campaign beverage. At home you can select a drink that is appropriate for any stage of a campaign. When the nominations are first made you are not excited and beer and cheese sandwiches seem to fit the case A little later, when the orators begin to come out into the open and shake their hair, you take cocktails and your eyes begin to resemble those of a caged rat, and you are ready to quarrel with an opponent. The next stage in the campaign is the whisky stage, and when you have got plenty of it the campaign may be said to be open, and you wear black eyes and lose your teeth, and you swear strange oaths and smell of kerosene, and only sleep in the morning. Then election comes and if your side wins you drink all kinds of things at once for a week, shout hoarsely and then go to the Keeley cure, but if your party loses you stay home and take a course of treatment for nervous prostration and say you will never mix up in another campaign.

Here in France it is different. The people have nervous prostration to start on, start a campaign on champagne, wind up on absinthe, and after the votes are counted go to an insane asylum. I do not know what first got dad to drink absinthe and I don't know what it is, but it looks like soap suds, tastes like seed cookies and smells like vermifuge. But it gets there just the same and the result of drinking it is about the same as the result of drinking anything in France—it makes you want to hug somebody.

At home when a man gets full of whisky, he wants to hug the man he drinks with and weep on his collar, and then hit him on the head with a bottle; but here every kind of drink puts the drinker in condition to want to hug. Dad says he never knew he had a brain until he learned to drink absinthe, but now he can close his eyes and see things worse than any mince pie nightmare, and when we go out among people he never sees a man at all, but when a woman passes along, dad's eyes begin to take turns winking at them and it is all I can do to keep him from proposing marriage to every woman he sees.

Badge on Dad's Breast, With the Word 'bishop' 153

I thought I would break him of this woman foolishness, so I told everybody dad was a Mormon bishop, and had a grand palace at Salt Lake City, and owned millions of gold mines and tabernacles and wanted to marry a thousand women and take them to Utah and place them at the head of homes of their own, and he would just call once or twice a week and leave bags of gold for his wives to spend. A newspaper reporter, that could talk English, wrote a piece for a paper about dad wanting to marry a whole lot and he said life in Utah was better than a Turkish harem, cause the wives of a Mormon bishop did not have to be locked up and watched by unix, but could flirt and blow in money and go out to dances and have just as much fun as though they lived in Newport, and had got divorces from millionaires, and he said any woman who wanted to marry a Mormon bishop could meet dad on the bullyvard near a certain monument, on a certain day. I was on to it, with the reporter, and we hired a carriage and went to the bullyvard, just at the time the newspaper said and I put a big red badge on dad's breast, with the word "Bishop" on it, and dad had been drinking absinthe and he thought the badge was a kind of sign of nobility. Well, you'd adide to see the bunch of women that were there to meet dad. "What's the matter here?" said dad, as he saw the crowd of women, looking like they were there in answer to an advertisement for nurses. I told dad to stand up in the carriage, like Dowie does in Chicago, and hold out his hands and say: "Bless you, my children," and when dad got up to bless them, the reporter and I got out of the carriage, and the reporter, which could talk French, said for all the women who wanted to be Mormon wives to get into the carriage with the bishop and be sealed for life.

Well, sir, you'd a thought it was a remnant sale! More than a dozen got into the carriage with dad, and about 400 couldn't get in, but when the scared driver started up the horses, they all followed the carriage, and then the mounted police surrounded the whole bunch and moved them off towards the police station, and dad under the wagonload of females, each one trying to get the nearest to him, so as to be his favorite wife.

It got noised around that a foreign potent-ate had been arrested with his whole harem for conduct unbecoming to a potent-ate, and so when we got to the jail dad had to be rescued from his wives, and they were driven into a side street by the police, and dad was locked up to save his life. The reporter and I went to the jail to get him out, but we had to buy a new suit of clothes for him, as everything was torn off him in the Mormon rush.

Dad Was a Sight when We Found Him in Jail 155

Dad was a sight when we found him in jail, and he thought his bones were broken, and he wanted to know what was the cause of his sudden popularity with the fair sex, and I told him it all came from his looking so confounded distinguished, and his flirting with women. He said he would swear he never looked at one of those women in a tone of voice that would deceive a Sunday school teacher, and he felt as though he was being misunderstood in France. We told him the only way to get out of jail was to say he was a crowned head from Oshkosh, traveling incog, and when he began to stand on his dignity and demand that a messenger be sent for the president of France, to apologize for the treatment he had received, the jailer and police begged his pardon and we dressed him up in his new clothes and got him out, and we went to the Eiffel tower to get some fresh air.

I suppose you have seen pictures of the Eiffel tower, on the advertisements of breakfast food in your grocery, but you can form no idea of the height and magnificence of the tower by studying advertisements. You may think that the pictures you see of world events on your cans of baked beans and maple syrup and soap, give you the benefit of foreign travel, but it does not. You have got to see the real thing or you are not fit to even talk about what you think you have seen. You remember that Ferris wheel at the Chicago world's fair, and how we thought it was the greatest thing ever made of steel, so high that it made us dizzy to look to the top of it, and when we went up on the wheel we thought we could see the world, from Alaska to South Africa, and we marveled at the work of man and prayed that we be permitted to get down off that wheel alive, and not be spilled down through the rarified Chicago atmosphere and flattened on the pavement so thin we would have to be scraped up off the pavement with a case knife, like a buckwheat cake that sticks to the griddle.

You remember, old man, how you cried when our sentence to ride in the Ferris wheel expired, and the jailer of the wheel opened the cell and let us out, and you said no one would ever get you to ride again on anything that you couldn't jump out of if it balked, or you got wheels in your head and chunks of things came up to your Adam's apple and choked you. Well, cross my heart, if that Ferris wheel, that looked so big to us, would make a main spring for the Eiffel tower. The tower is higher than a kite, and when you get near it and try to look up to the top, you think it is a joke, and that really no one actually goes up to the top of it. You see some flies up around the top of it, and when the guide tells you the flies crawling around there are men and women, you think the guide has been drinking.

Flies Crawling Around There Are Men and Women 157

But dad and I and the guide paid our money, got into an elevator and began to go up. After the thing had been going up awhile dad said he wouldn't go up more than a mile or so at first, and asked the man to let him off at the 3,000-foot level, but the elevator man said dad had got to take all the degrees and dad said: "Let her went," and after an hour or so we got to the top.

Gee! but I thought dad would fall dead right there, when he looked off at Paris and the world beyond. The flies we had seen at the top before starting had changed to human beings, all looking pale and scared, and the human beings on the ground had changed into flies and bugs, for all you could see of a man on the ground was his feet with a flattened plug hat someway fastened on the ankles, and a woman looked like a spoonful of raspberry jam dropped on the pavement, or a splash of current jelly moving on the ground in a mysterious way. I do not know as the Eiffel tower was intended to act as a Keeley cure, but of the 50 people who went up with us, half of them were so full their back teeth were floating, including dad and the guide, but when we got to the top and they got a view of the awful height to which we had come, it seemed as though every man got sober at once, and their tongues seemed to cleave to the roof of their mouths. All they could do was to look off at the city and the view in the distance, and choke up, and look sorry about something.

I couldn't help thinking of what sort of a pulp a man would be if he fell off the top of the tower and struck a fat woman on the pavement, cause it seemed to me you couldn't tell which was fat woman and which was man. I never saw such a change in a man as there was in dad, after he got his second wind and got his voice working. He looked like a man who had made up his mind to lead a different life and begin right there.

He Took out a Five-dollar Bill 159

There was a Salvation Army man and woman in the crowd and dad went up to them. He took out a five-dollar bill and put it in the tambourine of the lassie, and said to the man and woman: "Now, look a here, I want to join your church, and if you have got the facilities for giving me the degrees, you can sign me as a Christian right now. I have been a bad man, and never thought I needed the benefits of religious training, but since I got up here, so near Heaven, in an elevator which I will bet $10 will break and kill us all before we get down to Paris, I want you to prepare me for the hereafter quick."

Some of the other fellows laughed at dad, and the Salvation Army people looked as though dad was drunk, but he continued: "You can laugh and be jammed, but I'll never leave this place until I am a pious man, and you Salvation Army people have got to enlist me in your army, for I am scared plum to death. Go ahead and convert me, while we wait." The Salvation Army captain put his hand on dad's head, the girl held out the tambourine for another contribution, and dad felt a sweet peace come over him, and we went down in the elevator and took a hack to the hotel, and dad's lips worked as though in pain.

H.

CHAPTER XIII.

Monte Carlo.—Dear Uncle: I blush to write the name, Monte Carlo, at the head of a letter to anyone that is a Christian, or who believes in honesty and decency, and earning a living by the sweat of one's brow, for this place is the limit. If I should write anybody a letter from South Clark street, Chicago, the recipient would know I had gone wrong, and was located in the midst of a bad element, and the inference would be that I was the worst fakir, robber, hold-up man or assassin in the bunch.

The inference you must draw from the heading of this letter is that dad and I have taken all the degree of badness and are now winding up our career by taking the last degree, before passing in our chips and committing suicide. Do you know what this place is, old man? Monaco is a principality, about six miles square, ruled by a prince, and the whole business of the country, for it is a "country" the same as though it had a king, is gambling. They have all the different kinds of gambling, from chuck-a-luck at two bits to roulette at a million dollars a minute. What started dad to come to Monte Carlo is more than I know, unless it was a new American he has got acquainted with, a fellow from North Dakota, that dad met at a sort of dance that he did not take me to. It seems there is a place in Paris where they go to see men and women dance—one of those dances where they kick so high that their feet hit the gas fixtures.

Well, all I know about it is that one Wednesday night dad said he felt as though it was his duty to go to prayer meeting, so he could say when he got home that in all the frivolities of a trip abroad, even in wicked Paris, he never neglected his church duties. I never was stuck on going to prayer meeting, so dad let me stay at the hotel and play pool with the cash register boy in the barroom, and dad took a hymn book and went out, looking pious as I ever saw him.

Dance, Like They Had Seen the People Dance at The Show 164

My, what a difference there was in dad in the morning. I woke up about daylight, and dad came into the room with a strange man, with spinach on his chin, and they began to dance, like they had seen the people dance at the show where they had passed the evening. They were undressed, except their underclothes, which wore these combination suits, so when a man gets into them he is sealed up like a bologna, and he has to have help when he wants to get out to take a bath, and he has to have an outsider button him in with a button hook. Gee, I would rather be a sausage and done with it! Well, dad and this man from Dakota kicked high until dad caught by the ankle on a gas bracket, and the strange man got me up out of bed to help unloosen dad and get him down before he was black in the face. Finally we got dad down and then the two old codgers began to discuss a proposition to go to Monte Carlo to break the bank.

A System of Gambling 162

The Dakota man agreed that Americans had no right to be spending their own money doing Europe, when their genius was equal to the task of acquiring the money of the less intelligent foreigners. He said they could go to Monte Carlo and by a system of gambling which he had used successfully in the Black Hills they could carry away all the money they could pile into sacks. The man said he would guarantee to break the bank if dad would put his money against the Dakota man's experience as a gambler, and they would divide the proceeds equally. Dad bit like a bass. He said he had always had an element of adventure in his make-up, and had always liked to take chances, and from what he had heard of the fabulous sums won and lost at Monte Carlo he could see that if a syndicate could be formed that would win most of the time, he could see that there was more money in it than in any manufacturing enterprise, and he was willing to finance the scheme.

The Dakota man fairly hugged dad, and he told dad in confidence that they two could divide up money enough to make them richer than they ever dreamed of, and all the morning they discussed the plan, and made a list of things they would need to get away with the money. They provided themselves with canvas sacks to carry away the gold, and dad drew all his money out of the bank, and that evening we took a train for Monte Carlo. All the way here dad and his new friend chuckled over the sensation they would make among the gamblers, and I became real interested in the scheme. There was to be some fun besides the winning of the money, because they talked of going out in the park and on the terraces when they were tired of winning money, and seeing the poor devils who had gone broke commit suicide, as that is said to be one of the features of the place.

Seeing the Poor Devils Who Had Gone Broke 166

Well, we got a suite of rooms and the first day we looked over the place, and ate free banquets and saw how the people dressed, and just looked prosperous and showed money on the slightest provocation, and got the hang of things. Dad was to go in the big gambling room in the afternoon with his pockets fairly dropsical with money, and the Dakota man was to do the betting, and dad was to hold one of the canvas bags, and when it was full we were to take it to our room, and quit gambling for awhile, to give the bank a chance to raise more money. Dad insisted that his partner should lose a small bet once in awhile, so the bank should not get on to the fact that we had a cinch.

After luncheon we entered the big gambling room, in full-dress suits, and, by gosh! it was like a king's reception. There were hundreds of men and women, dressed for a party, and it did not seem like a gambling hell, except that there were, piles of gold as big as stoves, on all the tables, and the guests were provided with silver rakes, with long handles, to rake in the money. Dad said in a whisper to the Dakota man: "What is the use of taking the trouble to run a gold mine, and get all dirtied up digging dirty nuggets, when you can get nice, clean gold, all coined, ready to spend, by betting right?" And then dad turned to me and he said; "Hennery, don't let the sight of this wealth make you avaricious. Don't be purse-proud when you find that your poor father, after years of struggle against adversity, and the machinations of designing men, has got next to the Pierpont Morgan class and has money to buy railroads. Don't get excited when we begin to bag the money, but just act as though it was a regular thing with us to salt down our gold for winter, the same as we do our pork."

A count, or a duke, gave us nice seats, and rakes to haul in the money; a countess, with a low-necked dress, winked at dad when he reached into his pistol pocket and brought out a roll of bills and handed them to the Dakota man, who bought $500 worth of red chips, and when the man looked the roulette table over and put about a pint of chips on the red, dad choked up so he was almost black in the face, and began to perspire so I had to wipe my face with a handkerchief; the gambler rolled the wheel and when the ball stopped on the red, and dad did the raking and raked in a quart of chips, and dad shook hands with the Dakota man and said: "Pard, we have got 'em on the run," and reached for his sack to put in the first installment of acquired wealth, and the low-necked countess smiled a ravishing smile on dad, and dad looked as though he owned a brewery, and the Dakota man twisted his chin whiskers and acted like he was sorry for the Monte Carlo bank, I just got so faint with joy that I almost cried.

To think we had skinned along as economically as possible all our lives, and never made much money, and now, through this Dakota genius, and this Monte Carlo opportunity, we had wealth raking in by the bushel, made me feel great, and I wondered why more people had not found out this faraway place, where people could become rich and prosperous in a day, if they had the nerve. I tell you, old man, it was great, and I was going to cable you to sell out your grocery for what you could get at forced sale and come here with the money, gamble and become a millionaire.

Reach Into Another Pocket and Dig up Another Roll 171

Monte Carlo (the next day).—My Dear Uncle Ezra: I do not know how to write you the sequel to this tragedy. After our Dakota partner, with the Black Hills system of beating a roulette game, had won the first bet, he never guessed the right color again, and dad had no more use for the rake. Every time he bet and lost, he would reach out to dad for more money, and dad would reach into another pocket and dig up another roll, and the countess would laugh and dad had to act as though he enjoyed losing money.

It was about dark when dad had fished up the last hundred dollars and it was gone before dad could wink back to the countess, then the Dakota man looked at dad for more, and dad shook his head and said it was all off, and they looked it each other a minute, and then we all three got up and went out in the park to see the people who had gone broke commit suicide, but there was not a revolver shot and dad and the Dakota man sat down on a seat and I looked at the moon.

He would reach out to Dad for more money, and Dad would reach into another pocket and dig up another roll.

Dad looked at the Dakota man and said: "You started me in all right. What happened to your system?" The Dakota man was silent for a moment, and then he pointed to me and said: "That imp of yours crossed his fingers every time I bet, except the first time." Dad called me to him, and he said: "Hennery, let this be a lesson to you. Never to cross your fingers. You have ruined your dad," and he turned his pockets inside out, and hadn't change for a dollar note, and he gave me the empty sack to carry, and we went to our suite of rooms, knowing we would be fired out into the cold world.

It will take a week to get money from the states, and we may be sent to the work house, as we are broke, and haven't got the means even to commit suicide. Don't tell ma.

Yours,
Hennery.

CHAPTER XIV.

Geneva, Switzerland.—My Dear Old Man: By ginger, but I would like to be home now. I have had enough of foreign travel; I don't see what is the use of traveling, to see people of foreign countries, when you can go to any large city in America, and find more people belonging to any foreign country than you can find by going to that country, and they know a confounded sight more. Take the Russians in New York, the Norwegians of Minnesota, the Italians of Chicago, and the Germans of Milwaukee, and they can talk English, and you can find out all about their own countries by talking with them, but you go to their countries and the natives don't know that there is such a language as the United States language, and they laugh at you when you ask questions. I am sick of the whole business, and would give all I ever expect to be worth, to be home right now, with my skates sharp.

I would like to open the door of your old grocery, and take one long breath and die right there on the doorstep, rather than to live in luxury in any foreign country. Do you know, I sometimes go into a grocery store abroad, and smell around, in order to get my thoughts on dear old America, but nothing abroad smells as the same thing does in our country. If I could get one more smell of that keg of sauerkraut back of your counter, when it is ripe enough to pick, I think I would break right down and cry for joy. Of course I have smelled sauerkraut over here, but it all seems new and tame compared to yours. It may be the kraut here is not aged enough to be good, but yours is aged enough to vote and sticks to your clothes. Gee, but I just ache to get into your grocery and eat things, and smell smells, and then lay down on the counter with the cat with my head on a pile of wrapping paper and go to sleep and wake up in America, an American citizen, that no king or queen can tell to "hush up" and take off my hat when I want my hat on.

You may wonder how we got out of Monte Carlo, when we had lost every cent we had gambling. Well, we wondered about it all night, and had our breakfast sent up to our room, and had it charged, expecting that when the bill came in we would have to jump into the ocean, as we had no gun to kill ourselves with. Just after breakfast a duke, or something, came to our room, and dad said it was all off, and he called upon the Dakota man to make a speech on politics, while dad and I skipped out. We thought the duke, who was the manager of the hotel, would not understand the speech, and would think we were great people, who had got stranded.

Started in on a Democratic Speech 175

The Dakota man started in on a democratic speech that he used to deliver in the campaign of '96, and in half an hour the duke held up his hands, and the Dakota man let up on the speech. Then the duke took out a roll of bills and said: "Ze shentlemen is what you call bust. Is it not so?" Dad said he could bet his life it was so. Then the duke handed the roll of bills to dad, and said it was a tribute from the prince of Monaco, and that we were his guests, and when our stay was at an end, automobiles would be furnished for us to go to Nice, where we could cable home for funds, and be happy.

Well, when the duke left us, dad said: "Wouldn't that skin you?" and he gave the Dakota man one of the bills to try on the bartender, and when he found the money was good we ordered an automobile and skipped out for Nice. The chauffeur could not understand English, so we talked over the situation and decided that the only way to be looked upon as genuine automobilists would be to wear goggles and look prosperous and mad at everybody. We took turns looking mad at everybody we passed on the road, and got it down so fine that people picked up rocks after we had-passed, and threw them at us, and then we knew that we were succeeding in being considered genuine, rich automobile tourists.

After we had succeeded for an hour or two in convincing the people that we were properly heartless and purse proud, dad said the only thing we needed to make the trip a success was to run over somebody. He said nearly all the American automobile tourists in Europe had killed somebody and had been obliged to settle and support a family or two in France or Italy, and they were prouder of it than they would be if they endowed a university, or built a church, and he said he trusted our chauffeur would not be too careful in running through the country, but would at least cripple some one.

Well, just before we got to Nice, and darkness was settling down on the road, the chauffeur blew his horn, there was a scream that would raise hair on Horace Greeley's head, the automobile stopped, and there was a bundle of dusty old clothes, with an old woman done up in them, and we jumped out and lifted her up, and there we were, the woman in a faint, the peasants gathering around us with scythes and rakes and clubs, demanding our lives. The bloody-faced woman was taken into a home, the crowd held us, until finally a doctor came, and after examining the woman said she might live, but it would be a tight squeeze. We wanted to go on, but we didn't want to be cut open with a scythe, so finally a man, who said he was the husband of the woman, came out with a gun, dad got down on his knees and tried to say a prayer, the Dakota man held up both hands like it was a stage being held up, and I cried.

Dad Got Down on his Knees and Tried to Say a Prayer 178

Finally the chauffeur said, in broken English, that the husband would settle for $400, because he could pay the funeral expenses, get another wife for half the money and have some thing left to lay up for Christmas. As the man's gun was pointed at dad, he quit praying and gave up the money and agreed to send $50 a month for 11 years, until the oldest child was of age.

Well, we got away alive, got into Nice, and the chauffeur started back and we cabled home for money to be sent to Geneva, Switzerland. But, say; you have not heard the sequel. A story that has a sequel is always the best, and I hope to die if the police of Nice didn't tell us that we were buncoed by that old woman and that the chauffeur was in the scheme and got part of dad's money. The way they do it is to wait till dark, and then roll the woman in the dust and put some red ink on her face, and she pretends to be run over, and the doctor is hired by the month, and they average $500 a night, playing that game on automobile tourists from America. After the woman is run over every night, and the money is collected, and the victims have been allowed to go on their way, the whole community gathers at the house of the injured woman and they have a celebration and a dance, and probably our chauffeur got back to the house that night in time to enjoy the celebration. I suppose thousands of Americans are paying money for killing people that never got a scratch.

Say, we think in America that we have plenty of ways to rob the tenderfoot, but they give us cards and spades and little casino and beat us every time. Dad wanted to hire a hack and go back and finish that old woman with an ax, because he said he had a corpse coming to him, but the police told him he could be arrested for thinking murder, and that he was a dangerous man, and that they would give him 12 hours to get out of France, and so we bought tickets for Switzerland, though what we came here for I don't know, only dad said it was a republic like America and he wanted to breathe the free air of mountains in the home of the Switzerkase.

Well, anybody can have Switzerland if they want it. I will sell my interest cheap. The first three days we were here everybody wanted us to go out on the lake, said to be the most beautiful lake in the world, and we sailed on it, and rowed on it, and looked down into the clear water where it is said you can see a corpse on the bottom of the lake 100 feet down. We hadn't lost any corpse, except the corpse of that old woman we run over at Nice, but we wanted to get the worth of our money, so we kept looking for days, but the search for a corpse becomes tame after awhile, and we gave it up. All we saw in the bottom of the lake was a cow, but no man can weep properly over the remains of a cow, and dad said they could go to the deuce with their corpses, and we just camped at the hotel till our money came. Say, that lake they talk so much about is no better than lakes all over Wisconsin, and there are no black bass or muskellunges in it.

The tourists here are just daffy about climbing mountains and glaziers, and they talk about it all the time, and I could see dad's finish. They told him that no American that ever visited Switzerland would be recognized when he got home if he had not climbed the glaziers, so dad arranged for a trip up into the sky. We went 100 miles or so on the cars, passing along valleys where all the cows wear tea bells, and it sounds like chimes in the distance. It is beautiful in Switzerland, but the cheese is something awful. A piece of native Swiss cheese would break up a family.

At night we arrived at a station where we hired guides and clothes, and things, and the next morning we started. Dad wanted me to stay at the station a couple of days, while he was gone, and play with the goats, but I told him if there were any places in the mountains or glaziers any more dangerous than Paris or Monte Carlo, I wanted to visit them, so he let me go. Well, we were rigged up for discovering the north pole, and had alpenstocks to push ourselves up with, and the guides had ropes to pull us up when we got to places where we couldn't climb. I could get along all right, but they had dad on a rope most of the time pulling him until his tongue run out and his face turned blue. But dad was game, and don't you forget it.

Before noon we got on top of a glazier, which is the ice of a frozen river, that moves all the time, sliding towards the sea.

Dad Slipped Down a Crevice About 100 Feet

There was nothing but a hard winter, in summer, to the experience, and we would have gone back the same night, only dad slipped down a crevice about 100 feet with the rope on him, and the two guides couldn't pull him up, and we had to send a lunch down to him on the rope and one of the guides had to go back to the village for help to get dad up. Well, sir, I think dad was nearer dead than he ever was before, but they sent down a bottle of brandy, and when he drank some of it the snow began to melt and he was warm enough to use bad language.

He yelled to me that this was the limit and wanted to know how long they were going to keep him there. I yelled to him that one of the guides had gone for help to pull him out, and he said for them to order a yoke of oxen. I told him that probably he would have to remain there until spring opened and that I was going back to America and leave him there, and he better pray.

Have to Remain There Until Spring Opened 183

I don't know whether dad prayed, down there in the bowels of the mountains, but he didn't pray when help came, and they finally hauled him up. His breath was gone, but he gave those guides some language that would set them to thinking if they could have understood him, and finally we started down the mountain. They kept the rope on dad and every little while he would slip and slide 100 feet or so down the mountain on his pants, and the snow would go up his trousers legs clear to his collar, and the exercise made him so hot that the steam came out of his clothes, and he looked like a locomotive wrecked in a snow bank blowing off steam.

It became dark and I expected we would be killed, but before midnight we got to the station and changed our clothes and paid off the guides and took a train back. Dad said to me, as we got on the cars: "Now, Hennery, I have done this glazier stunt, just to show you that a brave man, whatever his age, is equal to anything they can propose in Europe, but by ginger, this settles it, and now I want to go where things come easier. I am now going to Turkey and see how the Turks worry along. Are you with me?" "You bet your life," says I.

Yours truly,
Hennery.

CHAPTER XV.

Venice, Italy.—My Dear Old Chumireno: Dad couldn't get out of Switzerland quick enough after he got thawed out the day after we climbed the glaziers. We found that almost all the tourists in Geneva were there because they did not want to go home and say they had not visited Switzerland, so they just jumped from one place to another. The people who stay there any length of time are like the foreign residents of Mexico, who are wanted for something they have done at home, that is against the law. There are more anarchists in Geneva than anything else, and they look hairy and wild eyed, and they plot to kill kings and drink beer out of two quart jars.

When we found that more attention was paid to men suspected of crime in their own countries, and men who were believed to be plotting to assassinate kings, dad said it would be a good joke if a story should get out that he was suspected of being connected with a syndicate that wanted to assassinate some one, so I told a fellow that I got acquainted with that the fussy old man that tried to ride a glazier without any saddle or stirrup was wanted for attempting to blow up the president of the United States by selling him baled hay soaked in a solution of dynamite and nitro-glycerine.

Dad and the Anarchists Reveled Till Morning 188

Say, they will believe anything in Switzerland. It wasn't two hours before long-haired people were inviting dad to dinners, and the same night he was taken to a den where a lot of anarchists were reveling, and dad reveled till almost morning. When he came back to the hotel he said his hosts got all the money he had with him, through some game he didn't understand, but he under stood it was to go into a fund to support deserving anarchists and dynamiters. He said when they found out he was a suspected assassin nothing was too good for him. He said they wanted to know how he expected to kill a president by soaking baled hay in explosives, and dad said it came to him suddenly to tell them that the president rode on horseback a good deal, and he thought if a horse was filled with baled hay, and nitro-glycerine and the president spurred the horse and the horse jumped in the air and came down kerchunk on an asphalt pavement, the horse would explode, and when the rider came down covered with sausage covers and horse meat, he would be dead, or would want to be. Dad said the anarchists went into executive session and took up a collection to send a man to Berlin to fill the emperor's saddle horse with cut feed like dad suggested.

Well, the anarchist story was too much for Switzerland, and the next morning dad was told by a policeman that he had to get out of the country quick, and it didn't take us 15 minutes to pack up, and here we are in Venice.

Well, say, old friend, this is the place where you ought to be, because nobody works here, that is, nobody but gondoliers. We have been here several days, and I have not seen a soul doing anything except begging, or selling things that nobody seems to want. If anybody buys anything but onions, it is for curiosity, or for souvenirs, and yet the whole population sits around in the sun and watches the strangers from other lands price things and go away without buying, and then everybody looks mad, as though they would like to jab a knife into the stranger. The plazas and the places near the canal are filled with hucksters and beggars, and you never saw beggars so mutilated and sore and disgusting. I never supposed human beings could be so deformed, without taking an ax to them, and it is so pitiful to see them that you can't help shedding your money.

Coughed up over $40 the First Day, Just Giving to Beggars

As hard hearted as dad is, he coughed up over $40 the first day, just giving to beggars, and he thought he had got them all bought up, and that they would let him alone, but the next day when he showed up there were ten beggars where there was one the day before, and they followed him everywhere, and all the loafers in the plazas laughed and acted as if they would catch the cripples when dad got out of sight and rob the beggars. Dad thinks the way the people live is by dividing with beggars. A man who has a deformity, or a sore that you can see half a block away, seems to be considered rich here, like a man in America who owns stock in great corporations. These beggars pay more taxes than the dukes and things who live in style.

I suppose dad never studied geography, so he didn't know how Venice was situated, so he told me to go out and order a hack the first morning we were here, and we would go and see the town. When I told dad there were no hacks, no horses and no roads in Venice, he said I was crazy in my head and wanted me to take some medicine and stay in bed for a few days, but I convinced him, when we got outdoors, that everything run by water, and when I showed him the canal and the gondolas, he remembered all about Venice, and picked out a gondalier that looked like one dad saw at the world's fair, and we hired him because he talked English. All the English the gondolier could use were the words "you bet your life," and "you're dam right," but dad took him because it seemed so homelike, and we have been riding in gondolas every day.

On the water you can get away from the beggars. This is an ideal existence. You just get in the gondola, under a canopy, and the gondolier does the work, and you glide along between build ings and wonder who lives there, and when they wake up, as all day long the blinds are closed, and everybody seems to be dead. But at night, when the canals are lighted, and the moon shines, the people put on their dress clothes and sit on verandas, or eat and drink, and talk Eyetalian, and ride in gondolas, and play guitars, and smoke cigarettes, and talk love. It is so warm you can wear your summer pants, and the water smells of clams that died long ago. It is just as though Chicago was flooded by the bursting of the sewers, and people had to go around State street, and all the cross streets, and Michigan avenue, in fishing boats, with three feet of water on top of the pavements. Imagine the people of Chicago taking gondolas and riding along the streets, landing at the stores and hotels, just as they do now from carriages.

We had been riding in gondolas for two days, getting around in the mud when the tide was out, and going to sleep and waiting for the tide to come in, when it seemed to me that dad needed some excitement, and last night I gave it to him.

We were out in our gondola, and the moon was shining, and the electric lights made the canal near the Rialto bridge as light as day. The Rialto bridge crosses the Grand canal, and has been the meeting place for lovers for thousands of years. It is a grand structure, of carved marble, but it wouldn't hold up a threshing machine engine half as well as an iron bridge. Well, the canal was filled with thousands of gondolas, loaded with the flower of Venetian society, and the music just made you want to fall in love. Dad said if he didn't fall in love, or something, before morning, he would quit the place. I made up my mind he should fall into something, so I began by telling dad it seemed strange to me that nobody but Eyetalians could run a gondola. Dad said he could run a gondola as well as any foreigner, and I told him he couldn't run a gondola for shucks, and he said he would show me, so he got out of the hen house where we were seated, and went back on to the pointed end of the gondola, and grabbed the pole or paddle from the gondolier, and said: "Now, Garibaldi, you go inside the pup tent with Hennery, and let me punt this ark around awhile."

Garibaldi thought dad was crazy, but he gave up the pole, and just then, when they were both on the extreme point of the gondola, and she was wabbling some, I peeked out through the curtains and thought the fruit was about ripe enough to pick, so I threw myself over to one side of the gondola, and, by gosh, if dad and Garibaldi didn't both go overboard with a splash, and one yell in the English language, and one in Eye-talian, and I rushed out of the cabin and such a sight you never saw.

Overboard, One Yell in the English Language, One In Eye-talian 193

Dad retained the paddle, and had his head out of water, but nothing showed above the water, where Garibaldi was except a red patch on his black pants. Dad was yelling for help, and finally the gondolier got his head out of the water, and said something that sounded like grinding a butcher knife on a grindstone, and I yelled, too, and the gondolas began to gather around us, and the two men were rescued. The gondolier had been gondoling all his life and he had never been in the water before, and they thought it would strike in and kill him, so they wrapped him up in blankets and put him aboard his canoe, and he looked at me as though I was to blame. They got a boat hook fastened in dad's pants and landed him in the gondola, and he dripped all the way to our hotel, and he smelled like a fish market.

I asked Garibaldi, on the way to the hotel, if he was counting his beads when he was down under the water with nothing but his pants out of the water, and he said: "You're dam right," but I don't think he knew the meaning of the words, because he probably wouldn't swear in the presence of death. Dad just sat and shivered all the way to the hotel, but when we got to our room I asked him what his idea was in jumping overboard right there before folks, with his best clothes on, and he said it was all Garibaldi's fault, that just as dad was getting a good grip on the paddle, the gondolier heaved a long sigh, and the onions in his breath paralyzed dad so he fell overboard.

Then You Don't Blame Your Little Boy, Do You 197

"Then you don't blame your little boy, do you?" says I, and dad looked at me as he was hanging his wet shirt on a chair. "Course not; you were asleep in the cabin. But say, if I ever hear that you did tip that gondola, it will go hard with you," but I just looked innocent, and dad went on drying his shirt by a charcoal brazier and never suspected me. But I am getting the worst of it, for dad and his clothes smell so much like a clam bake that it makes me sick.

Well, old friend, you ought to close up your grocery and come over here and go to Vesuvius and Pompeii with us, where we can dry our clothes by the volcano, and dig in the city that was buried in hot ashes 2,000 years ago. They say you can dig up mummies there that are dead ringers for you, old man.

  O, come on, and have fun with us.

  Your friend,

  Hennery.

CHAPTER XVI.

Naples, Italy.—Dear Old Partner in Crime: Well, sir, we have struck a place that reminds us of home, and your old grocery store. The day we got here dad and I took a walk into the poorer districts, where they throw all the slops and refuse in the streets, and where nobody ever seems to clean up anything and burn it. The odor was something that you cannot describe without a demonstration, and after we had turned pale and started to go away, dad said the smell reminded him of something at home, and finally he remembered your old grocery in the sauerkraut season, early in the morning, before you had aired out the place. Your ears must have burned when we were talking about you.

If you want to get an idea of Naples, at its worst, go down into your cellar and round up all the codfish, onions, kraut, limburger cheese, kerosene, rotten potatoes, and everything that is dead, put it all in a bushel basket, and just before the Health officers come to pull your place, get down on your knees and put your head down in the basket, and let some one sit on your head all the forenoon, and you will have just such a half day as dad and I had in the poor quarter of Naples, and it will not cost you half as much as it did us, unless, after you have enjoyed yourself in your cellar with your head in the basket, you decide to have a run of sickness and hire a doctor who will charge you the price of a trip to Europe.

Well, sir, Naples is a dandy, in its clean part. The bay of Naples is a dead ringer for Milwaukee bay, in shape and beauty, but Milwaukee lacks Vesuvius and Pompeii, for suburbs, and she lacks the customary highwaymen to hold you up. Every man, woman and child we have met makes a living out of the tourists, and nobody that I have seen works at any other business.

Wanted to Turn in a Fire Alarm 201

We woke up the first morning and dad looked out the window and saw Vesuvius belching forth flame and lava and stone fences, and wanted to turn in a fire alarm, but I told him that that fire had been raging ever since the Christian era, and was not one of these incendiary barn burnings, but he opened the window and yelled fire, and the porters and chambermaids came running to our room, with buckets of water, and wanted to know where the fire was. Dad pointed out of the window towards Vesuvius and said: "Some hired girl has been starting a fire with kerosene, in that shanty on the knoll out there, and the whole ranch will burn if you don't turn out the fire department, you gosh blasted lazy devils. Get a move on and help carry out the furniture."

Well, they calmed dad, and then I had to go to work and post dad up on the geography he had forgotten, and finally he remembered seeing a picture of a volcano or burning mountain in his geography 50 years ago, but he told me he never believed there was a volcano in the world, but that he always thought they put those pictures in geographies to make them sell. How a man can attain the prominence and position in the business world that dad has, and not know any more than he does, is what beats me.

Of course, you know, having kept a grocery since the war, and having had opportunities to study history, by the pictures on the soap boxes and insurance calendars, that Nero, the Roman tyrant, after Rome was burned, while he fiddled for a dance in a barn, got so accustomed to fire and brimstone that he retired to Naples and touched off Vesuvius, just so he could look at it. But Vesuvius, about 2,000 years ago, got to burning way down in its bowels, and the fire got beyond control, and I suppose now the fire is away down in the center of the earth, and you know when you get down in the earth below the crust, on which we live and raise potatoes, everything is melted, like iron in a foundry, and Vesuvius is the spigot through which the fluid comes to the surface. You see, don't you?

Just imagine that this earth is a barrel of beer, which you can understand better than anything else, and it is being shaken up by being hauled around on wagons and cars, and is straining to get out, then a bartender drives a spigot into the bung, turns the thumb piece, and the pent-up beer comes out foaming and squirting, and there you are.

Instead of beer, Vesuvius is loaded with lava, that runs like molasses, and when it is cold it is indigestible as a cold buckwheat cake, and you can make it up into jewelry, that looks like maple sugar and smells like a fire in a garbage crematory. Besides the lava there are stones as big as a house that are thrown up by the sea-sickness of the earth, as it heaves and pants, and then the ashes that come out of the crater at times would make you think that what they need there is to have a chimney sweep go down and brush out the flues.

Threw a Pail of Ashes over the Fence 204

To get an idea of what a nuisance the ashes from the crater are to the cities on the plain below, you remember the time you were out in your back yard splitting boxes for kindling wood and my chum and I threw a pail of ashes over the fence, and accidentally it went all over you, about four inches thick. That time you got mad and threw cucumbers at us, when we ran down the alley. Keep that in your mind and you can understand the destruction of Pompeii, when Vesuvius, thousands of years ago, coughed up hot ashes and covered the town 40 feet deep with hot stuff, and killed every living thing, and petrified and preserved the whole business, and made a prairie on top of a town, and everybody eventually forgot that there had ever been a town there, for about 2,000 years. If my chum and I had not run out of ashes we would have buried you so deep in your back yard that you would have been petrified with your hatchet, and when they excavated the premises a thousand years later they would have found your remains and put you in a museum.

Well, a couple of hundred years ago a peasant was sinking a well down in the ashes, and he struck a petrified barroom, with a bartender standing behind the bar in the act of serving some whisky 2,000 years old, and the peasant located a claim there, and the authorities took possession of the prairie and have been digging the town out ever since, looking for more of that 2,000-year-old whisky.

When I told dad about what they were finding at the ruins of Pompeii, and how you were liable to find gold and diamonds and petrified women, he wanted to go and dig in the ashes, as he said it would be more exciting than raking over the dumping grounds in Chicago for tin cans and lumps of coal, and so we hired a hack and went to the buried town, but dad insisted on carrying an umbrella, so if Vesuvius belched any more ashes he could protect himself. Gee, but from what I have seen at that old ruin, a man would need an umbrella made of corrugated iron to keep from being buried.

Dad Insisted on Carrying an Umbrella

Well, when we got to Pompeii dad was for going right where they were digging, but I got him to look over the streets and houses that had been uncovered first, and he was paralyzed to think that a town could be covered with ashes all these thousands of years, and then be uncovered and find a town that would compare, in many respects, with cities of the present day, with residences complete with sculpture, paintings and cut marble that would skin Chicago to a finish.

We went through residences that looked as rich as the Vanderbilt houses in New York, baths that you could take a plunge and a swim in, if they had the water, paintings that would take a premium at any horse show to-day, pavements that would shame the pavements of London and Paris, and petrified women that you couldn't tell from a low-necked party in Washington, except that the ashes had eaten the clothes off. I guess most of the people in Pompeii got away when the ashes began to rain down, for they must have seen that it wasn't going to be a light shower, but a deluge, 'cause they never have found many corpses. They must have run to Naples, and maybe they are running yet, and you may see some of them at your grocery, and if you do see anybody covered with ashes, looking for a job, give them some crackers and cheese and charge it to dad, for they must be hungry by this time.

Say, do you know that some of those refugees from Pompeii went off in such a hurry that they left bread baking in the ovens, and meat cooking in the pots? It seems the most wonderful thing to me of anything I ever saw. We went all through the streets and houses and saw ballrooms that beat anything in San Francisco, and when we went into a building occupied by the officers in charge of the excavations, and dad saw a telephone and an electric light, he thought those things had been dug up, too, and he claimed that the men who were receiving millions of dollars in royalties on telephones and electric lights were frauds who were infringing on Pompeii patents 2,000 years old, and he wouldn't believe me when I told him that telephones and electric lights were not dug up; he said then he wouldn't believe anything was dug up, but that the whole thing was a put-up job to rob tourists. But when we got to a locality where the dagoes were digging the ashes away from a house and were uncovering a parlor, where rich things were being discovered, he saw that it was all right.

I suppose I never ought to have played such a thing on dad, but I told him that anybody who saw a thing first when it came out of the ashes could grab it and keep it, and just as I told him a workman threw out a shovel full of ashes, just as you would throw out dirt digging for angle worms, and there was a little silver urn with a lot of coins in it, and you could not hold dad. He grabbed for it, the workman grabbed for it, and they went down together in the ashes, and the man rolled dad over and he was a sight, but the workman got the silver urn, and dad wanted to fight.

The Man Rolled Dad over and he Was a Sight

Finally a man with a uniform on came along and was going to arrest dad, but they finally compromised by the man offering to sell the silver urn and the gold coins to dad for a hundred dollars, if he would promise not to open it up until he got out of Italy, and dad paid the money and wrapped the urn up in a Chicago paper, and we took our hack and went back to Naples on a gallop.

Dad could hardly wait till we got to the hotel before opening up his prize, but he held out until we got to our room, when he unwrapped the urn to count his ancient gold coins. Well, you'd a-died to see dad's face when he opened that can. It was an old tomato can that had been wrought out with a hammer so it looked like hammered silver, and when he emptied the gold coins out on the table there was a lot of brass tags that looked like dog license tags, and baggage checks and brass buttons. I had to throw water on dad to bring him to, and then he swore he would kill the dago that sold him the treasure from the ruins of Pompeii. It was a great blow to dad, and he has bought a dirk knife to kill the dago. To-morrow we take in Vesuvius, and when we come down from the crater we go to Pompeii and kill the dago in his tracks. Dad may cause Vesuvius to belch again with hot ashes, and cover the ruins of Pompeii, but if he can't turn on the ashes, the knife will do the business.

Yours,
Hennery.

CHAPTER XVII.

Naples, Italy.—Siegnor ze Grocerino: I guess that will make you stand without hitching for a little while. Say, I am getting so full of dead languages, and foreign palaver, that I shall have to have an operation on my tongue when I get home before I can speel the United States language again so you can make head or tail of it. You see, I don't stay long enough in a country to acquire its language, but I get a few words into my system, so now my English is so mixed with French words, Italian garlic and German throat trouble that I cannot understand myself unless I look in a glass and watch the motions of my lips. Dad has not picked up a word of any foreign language, and says he should consider himself a traitor to his country if he tried to talk anything but English. He did get so he could order a glass of beer by holding up his finger and saying "ein," but he found later that just holding up his finger without saying "ein" would bring the beer all the same so he cut out the language entirely and works his finger until it needs a rest.

When I used to study my geography at the little red schoolhouse, and look at the picture of the volcano Vesuvius, and read about how it would throw up red-hot lava, and ashes, and rocks as big as a house, and wipe out cities, it looked so terrible to me that I was glad when we got through with the volcano lesson, and got to Greenland's icy mountains, where there was no danger except being frozen to death, or made sick by eating blubber sliced off of whales.

Then I never expected to be right on the very top of that volcano, throwing stones down in the lava, and sailing chips down the streams of hot stuff, just as I sailed chips on ice water at home-when the streets were flooded by spring rains. Say, there is no more danger on Vesuvius than there is in a toboggan slide, or shooting the chutes at home. I thought we would have to hire dagoes to carry us up to the top, and be robbed and held up, and may be murdered, but it is just as easy as going up in the elevator of a skyscraper, and no more terrifying than sitting on a 50-cent seat in a baseball park at home and witnessing the "Destruction of Pompeii" by a fireworks display

The crater looks sort of creepy, like a big cauldron kettle boiling soap on a farm, only it is bigger, and down in the earth's bowels you can well believe there is trouble, and if you believe in a hell, you can get it, illustrated proper, but the rivulets of lava that flow out of the wrinkles around the mouth of the crater are no more appalling than making fudges over a gas stove. When the lava cools you would swear it was fudges, only you can't eat the lava and get indigestion as you can eating fudges.

It was hard work to get dad to go up on the volcano, because he said he knew he would fall into it, and get his clothes burned, and he said he couldn't climb clear to the top, on account of his breath being short, but when I told him he could ride up on a trolley car, and have the volcano brought right to him, he weakened, and one morning we left Naples early and before two hours had passed we were on a little cogwheel railroad going up, and dad was looking down on the scenery, expecting every minute the cogs would slip and we would cut loose and go down all in a heap and be plastered all over the vineyards and big trees and be killed.

I don't know what makes dad so nervous, but he wanted a woman from Chicago, who was on the car with us, to hold his hand all the way up, but she said she was no nurse in a home for the aged, and she said she would cuff dad if he didn't let go of her. I told her she better not get dad mad if she knew what was good for her, for he was a regular Bluebeard, and wouldn't take no slack from no Chicago female, 'cause he had buried nine wives already. So she held his hand, and I guess she thinks she will be my stepmother, but I bet she don't.

Well, after we got almost to the top the car stopped, and we had to walk the rest of the way, several hundred feet, and we had to have a pusher and a putter for dad, a dago to go ahead and pull him up, and another to put his shoulder against dad's pants and shove. Gee, but it was a picture to see dad "go up old baldhead," with the dagoes perspiring and swearing at dad for being so heavy, and the Chicago woman laughing, and me pushing her up.

It Was a Picture to See Dad Go up Old Baldhead 214

One thing that scared dad was that every little way there was a shrine, where the guides left dad lying on the ground, blocked with a piece of cold lava, so he wouldn't roll down, like you would block a wagon wheel, and they would go to the shrine and kneel and say some prayers.

Dad was afraid they were going to charge the prayers in the bill for pushing him up, but I told dad that these people expected every time they, went up to the top that it would be their last trip, as they knew that some day the volcano would open in a new place and swallow them whole, with all the tourists. Then he gave them a dollar apiece to pray for him, and wanted to go back down the mountain and let Vesuvius run its own fireworks, but the Chicago lady told dad to brace up and she would protect him, and so the guides gave a few more pushes, and we were on top of the volcano, and dad collapsed and had to be brought to with smelling salts and whisky that the woman carried in her pistol pocket.

Gee, but it was worth all the trouble to get up the mountain, to see the sight that opened up. The hole in the mountain filled with boiling stuff was worth the price of admission, and the roaring of the boiling stuff, and the explosions way down cellar, and the flying stones, the smoke going into the air for a mile, like the burning of an oil well, the red-hot lava finding crevices to leak through, and flowing down the side of the mountain in streams like hot maple sirup, made a scene thai caused us to take off our hats and thank the good Lord that the thing hadn't overflowed enough to hurt us. But I could see dad was scared, 'cause when I wanted him to go around the edge of the crater with me, and see the hell-roaring free show from other points of view, and see where the hot ashes years ago rolled down and covered Pompeii and Herculaneum, he balked and said he had seen all he wanted to, and if he could stay alive until the next car went down the mountain, they could all have his interest in Vesuvius, and be darned to them, but he said if I wanted to go around looking for trouble, he would stay there under a big rock, with the Chicago lady, and wait for me to come back. She said she knew dad was all tired out, and needed rest, and she would stay with him, and keep him cheered up; so I left them and went off with one of the dagoes, to slide down hill on some flowing lava, and pick up specimens.

Well, sir, I wish I could get along some way without telling the rest of this sad story, but if I am going to be a historian I have got to tell the whole blame thing.

And She Was Stroking his Hair 217

When I left dad and the Chicago woman she had produced a lunch from somewhere about her person, and a small bottle, and they were eating and drinking, and dad was laughing more natural than I had seen him laugh since we run over the old woman with the automobile at Nice, and she was smiling on dad just as though she was his sweetheart. (As I went around the crater, a couple of blocks away, I looked back and dad had laid his head in her lap, and she was stroking his hair.)

Well, I picked up specimens, burned the soles off my shoes wading in the lava, and took in the volcano from all sides, and after an hour I went back to where dad and the woman were lunching, but the woman was gone, and dad acted as though he had been hit by an express train, his eyes were wild, his collar was gone, his pocketbook was on the ground, empty, his coat was gone, his scarf-pin had disappeared and the $11 watch he bought when he was robbed the other time was missing, and dad's tongue was run out, and he was yelling for water. I thought he had been trying to drink some lava.

He Was Yelling for Water 223

"Dad, what in the world has happened to you?" said I, as I rushed up to him.

"That woman has happened to me, that is all," said dad, as he took a swallow of water out of a canteen one of the dagoes had.

"Tell me about it, dad," said I, trying to keep from laughing, when I saw that he was not hurt.

"Say, let this be a lesson to you," said dad, "and don't you steer another woman to me on this trip. Do you know you hadn't more than got around that big rock when she said she was tired and was going to faint, for the altitude was too high for her, and I tried to soothe her, and she did look pale, and, by gosh, I thought she was going to die on my hands, and I would have to carry her corpse down the mountain. I heard a scuffling on the rocks, and she looked up and saw a man not ten feet away, and she said: 'Me husband!' and then she fainted and grabbed me around the neck, and I couldn't get her loose. She just froze to me like a person drowning, and that husband of hers, who had come up on the last car, hunting for his wife, who had eloped, pulled a long blue gun and told me he would give me five minutes to pray, and then he would kill me and throw my body down in the creater, to sizzle."

Pulled a Long Blue Gun 220

"I told him I could pay up enough ahead in three minutes, and he could take all I had if he would loosen up his wife, and bring her to, and take her away, and let me die all alone, and let the buzards eat me, uncooked. He took the bet, pulled her arms away from my throat, took my money and coat, brought her to, and said he was going to throw her into the crater, but I told him she had certainly been good to me, and if he would spare her life, and take her away in the cars, he could have my watch and scarfpin, and he took them, and they went to the cars.

"She looked back at me with the saddest face I ever saw, and said: 'O, sir, it is all a terrible dream, and I will see you in Naples, and explain all,' and now, by Christmas, I want to go back to town and find her, and rescue her from that jealous husband," and dad got up and we started for the car.

The man and his wife went down on the car ahead of us, and dad wouldn't believe they were regular bunko people, who play that game everyday on some old sucker, but the man that runs the car told me so.

I can be responsible for dad in everything except the women he meets. When it comes to women, your little Hennery don't know the game at all.

Yours,
Hennery.

CHAPTER XVIII.

Rome, Italy.—My Dear Old "Pard:" Well, sir, if you could see me now, you wouldn't know me, because foreign travel has broadened me out so I can talk on any subject, and people of my age look upon me as an authority, and they surround me everywhere I go and urge me to talk. The fact that the boys and girls do not understand a word I say makes no difference. They do not wear many clothes here, and there is no style about them, and when they see me with a whole suit of clothes on, and a hat and shoes and socks, and a scarf-pin on my necktie, they think I must be an Americano that is too rich for any use, or something that ranks with a prince at least, and the boys delight to be with me and do errands for me, and the girls seem to be in love with me.

There is no way you can tell if a girl is in love with you, except that she looks at you with eyes that are as black as coal, and they seem to burn a hole right into your insides, and when they take hold of your hand they hang on and squeeze like alamand-left in a dance at home, and they snug up to you and are as warm and cheerful as a gas stove.

It Brought on a Revolution 227

Say, I sat on a bench in a plaza with a girl about my age, for an hour, while the other girls and boys sat on the ground and looked at us in admiration, and when I put my arm around her and kissed her on her pouting lips, it brought on a revolution. An Italian soldier policeman took me by the neck and threw me across the street, the girl scratched me with her finger nails and bit me, and yelled some grand hailing sign of distress, her brother and a ragged boy that was in love with the girl and was jealous, drew daggers, and the whole crowd yelled murder, and I started for our hotel on a run, and the whole population of Rome seemed to follow me, and I might as well have been a negro accused of crime in the states. I thought they would burn me at the stake, but dad came out of the hotel and threw a handful of small change into the crowd, and it was all off.

After they picked up the coin they beckoned me to come out and play some more, but not any more for little Hennery. I have been in love in all countries where we have traveled, and in all languages, but this Italian love takes the whole bakery, and I do not go around any more without a chaperone. The girls are ragged and wear shawls over their heads, and there are holes in their dresses and their skin isn't white, like American girls', but is what they call olive complexion, like stuffed olives you buy in bottles, stuffed with cayenne pepper, but the girls are just like the cayenne pepper, so warm that you want to throw water on yourself after they have touched you. Gee, but I wouldn't want to live in a climate where girls were a torrid zone, 'cause I should melt, like an icicle that drops in a stove, and makes steam and blows up the whole house.

Well, old man, you talk about churches, but you don't know anything about it. Dad and I went to St. Peter's in Rome, and it is the grandest thing in the world. Say, the Congregational church at home, which we thought so grand, could be put in one little corner of St. Peter's, and would look like 30 cents. St. Peter's covers ground about half a mile square, and when you go inside and look at grown people on the other side of it, they look like flies, and the organ is as big as a block of buildings in Chicago, and when they blow it you think the last day has come, and yet the music-is as sweet as a melodeon, and makes you want to get down on your knees with all the thousands of good Christians of Italy, and confess that you are a fraud that ought to be arrested.

Dad and I have been to all kinds of churches, everywhere, and never turned a hair, but since we got to this town and got some of the prevailing religion into our systems, we feel guilty, and it seems as though everybody could see right into us, and that they knew we were heathen that never knew there was a God. Sure thing, I never supposed there were so many people in the world that worshiped their Maker, as there are here, and I don't wonder that all over the world good people look to Rome for the light. Dad keeps telling me that when we get home we will set an example that will make people pay attention, but he says he does not want to join the church until he has seen all the sights, and then he will swear off for good.

He said to me yesterday: "Now, Hennery, I have been to all the pious places with you, the pope's residence, the catacombs and St. Peter's, where they preach from 40 different places and make you feel like giving up your sins, and I have looked at carvings and decorations and marble and jewels and seen the folly of my ways of life, and I am ripe for a change, but before I give up the world and all of its wickedness, I want blood. I want to go to the other extreme, and see the wild beasts at the Coliseum tear human beings limb from limb, and drink their blood, and see gladiators gladiate, and chop down their antagonists, and put one foot on their prostrate necks, like they do in the theaters, and then I am ready to leave this town and be good."

Well, sir, I have been in lots of tight places before, but this one beat the band. Here was my dad, who did not know that the Roman, gladiator business had been off the boards for over 2,000 years, that the eating of human prisoners by wild beasts in the presence of the Roman populace was played out, and that the Coliseum was a ruin and did not exist as a place of amusement. He thought everything that he had read about the horrors of a Roman holiday was running to-day, as a side show, and he wanted to see it, and I had encouraged him in his ideas, because he was nervous, and I didn't want to undeceive him. He had come to Rome to see things he couldn't find at home, and it was up to me to deliver the goods.

Gee, but it made me sweat, 'cause I knew if dad did not get a show for his money he would lay it up against me, so I told him we would go to the Coliseum that night and see the hungry lions and tigers eat some of the leading citizens, just as they did when Caesar run the show. Then I found an American from Chicago at the hotel, who sells soap in Rome, and told him what dad expected of me in the way of amusement, and he said the only way was to take dad out to the Coliseum, and in the dark roll a barrel of broken glass down the tiers of seats and make him believe there was an earthquake that had destroyed the Coliseum, and that the lions and tigers were all loose, looking for people to eat, and scare dad and make a run back to town.

What Dad Expected of Me in the Way Of Amusement 230

I didn't want to play such a scandalous trick on dad, but the Chicago man said that was the only way out of it, and he could get a barrel of broken glass for a dollar, and hire four ruffians that could roar like lions for a few dollars, and it would give dad good exercise, and may be save him from a run of Roman fever, 'cause there was nothing like a good sweat to knock the fever out of a fellow's system. The thing struck me as not only a good experience for dad, but a life saver, so I whacked up the money, and the Chicago soap man did the rest.

After dark we went out to the ruin of the Coliseum, where a great many tourists go to look at the ruins by moonlight, and dad was as anxious and bloodthirsty as a young surgeon cutting up his first "stiff." When we got to the right place, and I told dad we were a little early, because the nobility were not in their seats, the villains began to roar three dollars' worth like hungry lions, and dad turned a little pale and said that sounded like the real thing.

I told him we better not get too near, because we were not accustomed to seeing live men chewed up by beasts, and dad said he didn't care how near we got, as long as they chewed and tore to pieces the natives; so we started to work up a little nearer, when there was a noise such as I never heard before, as the hogshead of broken glass began to roll down the tiers of stone seats, and I fell over on the ground, and pushed dad, and he went over in the sand and struck his pants on a cactus, and yelled that he was stabbed with a dirk.

Went over in the Sand and Struck his Pants on a Cactus 233

I got up and fell down again, and just then the Chicago soap man came up on a gallop, followed by the villains playing lion and tiger, and dad asked the Chicago man what seemed to be the matter, and he said: "Matter enough; there has been an earthquake, and the Coliseum has fallen down, killing more than 10,-000 Romans, and the animals' cages are busted and the animals are loose, looking for fresh meat, and we better get right back to Rome, too quick, or we will be eaten alive. Come on if you are with me. Do you hear the lions after us?" said he, as the hired villains roared.

He Took the Lead for Good Old Rome 235

Well, you'd a died to see dad get up out of that prickly cactus and take the lead for good old Rome. I didn't know he was such a sprinter, but we trailed along behind, roaring like lions and snarling like tigers and yip-yapping like hyenas and barking like timber wolves, and we couldn't see dad for the dust, on that moonlight night.

We slowed up and let dad run ahead, and he got to the hotel first, and we paid off the villains, and finally we went in the hotel and found dad in the bar-room puffing and drinking a high-ball. "Pretty near hell, wasn't it," said dad, to the soap man. "Did the lions catch anybody?" "O, a few of the lower classes," said the soap man, "but none of the nobility. The nobility were in the boxes and that part of the Coliseum never falls during an earthquake," and the soap man joined dad in a high-ball.

After dad got through puffing and had wiped about two quarts of perspiration off his head and neck, and the soap man had told him what a great thing it was to perspire in Rome, on account of the Roman fever, that catches a man at night and kills him before morning, dad turned to me and said: "Hennery, you go pack up and we get out of this in the morning, for I feel as though I had been chewed by one of those hyenas. Not any more Rome for papa," and the high-ball party broke up, and we went to bed to get sleep enough to leave town.

Do you know, the next morning those hired villains made the soap man and I pay ten dollars extra on account of straining their lungs roaring like lions? But we paid for their lungs all right, rather than have them present a bill to dad.

Well, good-by, old man. We are getting all the fun there is going.

Your only,
Hennery.

CHAPTER XIX.

Rome, Italy.—Dear Old Friend: You remember, don't you when you were a boy, playing "tag, you're it," and "button, button, who's got the button?" that one of the trying situations was to be judged to "go to Rome," which meant that you were to kiss every girl in the room.

Had to Kiss Anybody They Brought To Me 238

I never got enough "going to Rome" when I attended church sociables and parties, but always got blindfolded, and had to kiss anybody they brought to me, which was usually a boy or a colored cook, so I teased dad to take me to Rome, and when he got over his being rattled and robbed and burned by lava at Vesuvius, he said he didn't care where he went, and, besides, I told him about the Roman Coliseum, where they turned hungry tigers and lions and hyenas loose among the gladiators, and the people could see the beasts eat them alive, and dad said that was something like it, as the way he had been robbed and misued in Italy, he would enjoy seeing a good share of the population chewed by lions, if the lions could stand it. I didn't tell dad that the wild animal show had not been running for a couple of thousand years, 'cause I thought he would find it out when we got here.

Say, old man, I guess I can help you to locate Rome. You remember the time I spoke a piece at the school exhibition, when I put my hand inside my flannel shirt, like an orator, and said: "And this is Rome, that sat on her seven hills, and from her throne of beauty ruled the whole world." Well, this is it, where I am now, but the seven hills have been graded down, and Rome don't rule the whole world a little bit; but she has got religion awful.

The pope lives here, and he is the boss of more religious people than anybody, and though you may belong to any other kind of church, and when you are home you don't care a continental for any religion except your own, or your wife's religion, and you act like an infidel, and scoff at good people, when you get to Rome and see the churches thicker than saloons in Milwaukee, and everybody attending church and looking pious, you catch the fever, and try to forget bad things you have done, and if you get a chance to see the pope, you may go to his palace just 'cause you want to see everything that is going on, and you think you don't care whether school keeps or not, and you feel independent, as though this religion was something for weak people to indulge in, and finally you come face to face with the pope, and see his beautiful face, and his grand eyes, and his every movement is full of pious meaning, you "penuk" right there, and want to kneel down and let him bless you, by gosh.

Say, I never saw dad weaken like he did when the pope came in. We got tickets to go to his reception, but dad said he had rather go to the catacombs, or the lion show at the Coliseum. He said he didn't want to encourage popes, because he didn't believe they amounted to any more than presiding elders at home. He said he had always been a Baptist, and they didn't have any popes in his church, and he didn't believe in 'em, but some other Americans were going to see the pope, and dad consented to go, under protest, it being understood that he didn't care two whoops, anyway.

Well, sir, we went, and it was the grandest thing you ever saw. There were guards by the thousand, beautiful gardens that would make Central Park look like a hay marsh, hundreds of people in church vestments, and an air of sanctity that we never dreamed; jewels that are never seen outside the pope's residence, and we lined up to see the holy father pass.

Gee, but dad trembled like a dog tied out in the snow, and the perspiration stood out on his face, and he looked sorry for himself. Then came the procession, all nobles and great people, and then there was a party of pious men carrying the most beautiful man we ever saw on a platform above us, and it was the pope, and he smiled at me, and the tears came to my eyes, and I couldn't swallow something which I s'pose was my sins, and then he looked at dad, and held up one hand, and dad was pale, and there was no funny business about dad any more, and then they set the platform down and the pope sat in a chair, and those who wanted to went up to him, and he blessed them.

For Awhile Dad Dassent Go up 241

Say, for awhile dad dassent go up, 'cause he thought the pope could see right through him, and would know he was a Baptist, but the rest of the Americans were going up, and dad didn't want to be eccentric, so he and I went up. The pope put out his hand to dad, and instead of shaking it, as he would the hand of any other man on earth, and asking how his folks were, dad bent over and kissed the pope's hand, and the pope blessed him. Dad looked like a new man, a good man, and when the pope put his hand on my head, and blessed me, my heart came up in my throat, 'cause I thought he must know of all the mean things I had ever done, but I can feel his soft, beautiful hand on my head now, and from this out I would fight any boy twice my size that ever said a word against the pope and his religion. When we got outside dad says to me: "Hennery, don't you ever let me hear of your doing a thing that would make the good man sorry if he was to hear about it." And we went to our hotel and stayed all the afternoon, and all night, and just thought of that pope's angelic face, and when one of the Americans came to our room and wanted dad to play cinch, he was indignant, and said: "I would as soon think of robbing a child's bank," and we went to bed, and if dad wasn't a converted man I never saw one.

Well, sir, trouble, and sorrow, and religion, don't last very long on dad. The next morning we talked things over, and I quoted all the Roman stuff I could think of to dad, such as "In that elder day, to be a Roman was greater than a king," but before I could think twice there was a commotion in the streets and a porter came and made us take off our hats, because the king was riding by, and we looked at the king, and dad was hot. He said that fellow was nothing but a railroad hand, disguised in a uniform, and, by ginger, if we had seen that king out west working on a railroad, with canvas clothes on, he would not have looked like a king, on a bet. There was nothing but his good clothes that stood between the king and a dago digging sewers in Chicago.

After the king and his ninespots had passed, dad said: "When you are in Rome, you must do as the Romans do," and he said he wanted to get that heavy feeling off his shoulders, which he got at the religious procession, and wanted me to suggest something devilish that we could do, and I told him we better go and see the "Catacombs." He wanted to know if it was anything like "a trip to Chinatown," or the "Black Crook," and I told him it was worse. Then he asked me if there was much low neck and long stockings in the "Catacombs," and I told him there was a plenty, and he said he was just ripe to see that kind of a show, and so we took a carriage for the "Catacombs," and dad could hardly keep still till we got there.

I suppose I ought to be killed for fooling dad, but he craved for excitement, and he got it. The "Catacombs" are where Roman citizens have been buried for thousands of years, in graves hewn out of solid rock, and they are petrified, and after they have laid in the graves for a few hundred years, the mummified bodies are taken out and stood up in corners, if the bodies will hang together, and if not the bones are piled up around for scenery.

We had to take torches to go in, and we wandered through corridors, gazing at the remains, until dad asked one of the men with us what it all meant, and the man said it was the greatest show on earth. Dad began to think he was nutty, and when I laughed, and said: "That is great," and clapped my hands, and said: "Encore," dad stopped and said: "Hennery, this is no leg show, this is a morgue," but to cheer him up I told him his head must be wrong, and I pointed to about a hundred dried corpses, a thousand years old, in a corner, with grinning skulls all around, and told him that was the ballet, and told him to look at the leading dancer, and asked him if she wasn't a beaut, from Butte, Mont., and that killed dad. He leaned against me, and said his eyes must have gone back on him, because everything looked dead to him. I told him he would get over it after awhile, and to stay where he was while I went and spoke to one of the ballet that was beckoning to me, and I left him there, dazed, and went around a corner and hid.

People were coming along with torches all the time, looking at the catacombs and reading the inscriptions cut in the rock, and after awhile I went back to where I left dad, and he was gone, but after awhile I found him standing up with the stiffs. He was glad to see me, and wanted to know if I thought he was' dead. I told him I was sure he was alive, though he had a deathly look on his face.

He Would Break Me up Into Bones, and Throw Me Into a Pile 246

"Well, sir," says dad, "I thought it was all over with me, after you left, for a man came along and moved me around, and took hold under my arms and jumped me along here by these stiffs, and told me if I didn't stay where I belonged he would break me up into bones, and throw me into a pile, and I thought I would have to do as the Romans do and stay here, and before the man left me he reached into my pocket and took my money, and said I couldn't spend any money in there where I was going to stay for a million years, and, by gosh, I was so petrified I couldn't stop him from robbing me. Say, Hennery, they will rob you anywhere, even in the grave, and if this Catacomb show is over, and the curtain has gone down, I want to get out of here, and go to the Coliseum or the Roman amphitheater, where the wild beasts eat people alive." And so we left the Catacombs and went back to town, and dad began to show life again. Say, you tell the folks at home that dad is gaining every day, and his vacation is doing him good. He has promised to kill me for taking him to the Catacomb show, but dad never harbors revenge for long, and I guess your little nephew will pull through. I wish I had my skates, cause dad wants to go to Russia.

Yours,
Hennery.

CHAPTER XX.

St. Petersburg, Russia.—My Dear Groceryow-ski: Well, sir, I 'spose you will be surprised to hear from me in Russia, but there was no use talking when Dad said he was going to St. Petersburg if it was the last act of his life. He got talking with a Japaneser in Rome and the Jap said the war in the far east would last until every Russian was killed, unless America interfered to put a stop to it, and as Roosevelt didn't appear to have sand enough to offer his services to the czar, what it needed was for some representative American citizen who was brave and had nerve to go to St. Petersburg and see the czarovitch and give him the benefit of a good American talk. The Jap said the American who brought about peace, by a few well chosen remarks, would be the greatest man of the century, and would live to be bowed down to by kings and emperors and all the world would doff hats to him.

At first dad was a little leary about going on such a mission without credentials from Washington, but as luck would have it, he met an exiled Russian at a restaurant, who told dad that he reminded him of Gen. Grant, because dad had a wart on the side of his nose, and he told dad that Russia would keep on fighting until every Japanese was killed unless some distinguished American should be raised up who deemed it his duty to go to St. Petersburg and see the Little Father, and in the interest of humanity advise the czar to call a halt before he had exterminated the whole yellow race. Dad asked the Russian if he thought the czar would grant an audience to an American of eminence in his own country, and the Russian told dad that Nicholas just doted on Americans, and that there was hardly ever an American ballet dancer that went to Russia but what the czar sent for her to come and see him and dance before the grand dukes, and he always gave them jewels and cans of caviar as souvenirs of their visit.

The Russian Told Dad That Nicholas Just Doted On Americans 250

Dad thought it over all night, and the next morning we started for Russia and I wish we had joined an expedition to discover the North Pole instead of coming here. Say, it is harder to get into Russia than it would be to get out of a penitentiary at home. At the frontier we were met by guards on horseback and on foot, policemen, detectives and other grafters, who took our passports and money, and one fellow made me exchange my socks with him. Then they imprisoned us in a stable with some cows until they could hold a coroner's inquest on our passports and divide our money. We slept with the cows the first night in Russia, and I do not want to sleep again with animals that chew cuds all night, and get up half a dozen times to hump up their backs and stretch and bellow. We never slept a wink, and could look out through the cracks in the stable and see the guards shaking dice for our money.

See the Guards Shaking Dice for Our Money 253

Finally they looked at the great seal on our passports and saw it was an American document, and they began to turn pale, as pale as a Russian can get without using soap, and when I said, "Washington, embassador, minister plenipotentiary, Roosevelt, Hot Time in the Old Town Tonight, E Pluribus Unum, whoopla, San Juan Hill," and pointed to dad, who was just coming out of the stable, looking like Washington at Valley Forge, the guards and other robbers bowed to dad, gave him a bag full of Russian money in place of that which they had taken away, and let us take a freight train for St. Petersburg, and they must have told the train men who we were, because everybody on the cars took off their hats to us, and divided their lunch with us.

Dad could not understand the change in the attitude of the people towards us until I told him that they took him for a distinguished American statesman, and that as long as we were in Russia he must try to look like George Washington and act like Theodore Roosevelt, so every little while dad would stand up in the aisle of the car and pose like George Washington and when anybody gave him a sandwich or a cigarette he would show his teeth and say, "Deelighted," and all the way to St. Petersburg dad carried out his part of the programme and we were not robbed once on the trip, but dad tried to smoke one of the cigarettes that was given him by a Cossack, and he died in my arms, pretty near.

They make cigarettes out of baled hay that has been used for beddings and covered with paper that has been used to poison flies. I never smelled anything so bad since they fumigated our house by the board of health after the hired girl had smallpox.

Well, we got to St. Petersburg in an awful time, and went to a hotel, suspected by the police, and marked as undesirable guests by the Cossacks, and winked at by the walking delegates and strikers, who thought we were non-union men looking for their jobs.

The next day the religious ceremony of "blessing the Neva" took place, where all the population gets out on the bank of the river, with overshoes on, and fur coats, and looks down on the river, covered with ice four feet thick, and the river is blessed. In our country the people would damn a river that had ice four feet thick, but in Russia they bless anything that will stand it. We got a good place on the bank of the river, with about a million people who had sheepskin coats on, and who steamed like a sheep ranch, and were enjoying the performance, looking occasionally at the Winter palace, where the czar was peeking out of a window, wondering from which direction a bomb would come to blow him up, when a battery of artillery across the river started to fire a salute, and then the devil was to pay. It seems that the gentlemen who handled the guns, and who were supposed to fire blank cartridges into the air, put in loaded cartridges, filled with grape shot, and took aim at the Winter palace, and cut loose at Mr. Czar.

Well, you would have been paralyzed to see the change that came over that crowd, blessing the river one minute and damning the czar and the grand dukes the next. The shot went into the Winter palace and tore the furniture and ripped up the ceiling of the room the czar was in, and in a moment all was chaos, as though every Russian knew the czar was to be assassinated at that particular moment, and all rushed toward the Winter palace as though they expected pieces of the Little Father would be thrown out the window for them to play football with. For a people who are supposed to be lawful and law-abiding, and who love their rulers, it seemed strange to see them all so tickled when they thought he was blown higher than a kite by his own soldiers.

Dad and I started with the crowd for the Winter palace, and then we had a taste of monarchial government. The crowd was rushing over us and dad got mad and pulled off his coat and said he could whip any confounded foreigner that rubbed against him with a sheepskin coat on, and he was just on the point of smiting a fellow with whiskers that looked like scrambled bristles off a black hog when a regiment of Cossacks came down on the crowd, riding horses like a wild west show, and with whips in their hands, with a dozen lashes to each whip, and they began to lash the crowd and ride over them, while the people covered their faces with their arms, and run away, afraid of the whips, which cut and wound and kill, as each lash has little lead bullets fastened to them and a stroke of the whip is like being shot with buck shot or kicked with a frozen boot.

A Cossack Rode Right up to Him and Lashed Him over The Back 258

Well, sir, dad was going to show the Cossacks that he was pretty near an American citizen and didn't propose to be whipped like a school boy by a teacher that looked like a valentine, so he tried to look like George Washington defying the British, but it didn't work, for a Cossack rode right up to him and lashed him over the back (and about 15 buck shot in his whip took dad right where the pants are tight when you bend over to pick up something) and the Cossack laughed when dad straightened up and started to run. I never saw such a change in a man as there was in dad. He started for our hotel, and as good a sprinter as I am I couldn't keep up with him, but I kept him in sight. Before we got to the hotel a sledge came along, not an "old sledge," such as you play with cards, high-low-Jack-game, but a sort of a sleigh, with three horses abreast, and I yelled to dad to take a hitch on the sledge, and he grabbed on with his feet on the runners, and a man in the sledge with a uniform on, who seemed to be a grand duke, 'cause everybody was chasing him and yelling to head him off, hit dad in the nose with the butt of a revolver, and dad fell off in the snow and the crowd that was chasing the grand duke picked dad up and carried him on their shoulders because they thought he had tried to assassinate the duke, and we were escorted to our hotel by the strikers.

Hit Dad in the Nose With The Butt of a Revolver 255

We didn't know what they were, but you can tell the laboring men here because they wear blouses and look hungry, and when they left us the landlord notified the police that suspicious characters were at the hotel, and came there escorted by the mob, and the police surrounded the house and dad went to our room and used witch hazel on himself where the Cossack hit him with the loaded whip. He says Russia will pay pretty dear for that stroke of the whip by the Cossack, and I think dad is going to join the revolution that is going to be pulled off next Sunday.

They are going to get about a million men to take a petition to the czar, workingmen and anarchists, and dad says he is going as an American anarchist who is smarting from injustice, and I guess no native is smarting more than dad is, 'cause he has to stand up to eat and lie on his stummick to sleep. There is going to be a hades of a time here in St. Petersburg this next week, and dad and I are going to be in it clear up to our necks.

Dad has given up trying to see the czar about stopping the war and says the czar and the whole bunch can go plum (to the devil) and he will die with the mob and follow a priest who is stirring the people to revolt.

Gee, I hope dad will not get killed here and be buried in a trench with a thousand Russians, smelling as they do.

I met a young man from Chicago, who is here selling reapers for the harvester trust, and he says if you are once suspected of having sympathy with the working people who are on a strike you might just as well say your prayers and take rough on rats, 'cause the Cossacks will get you, and he would advise me and dad to get out of here pretty quick, but when I told dad about it he put one hand on his heart and the other on his pants and said "Arnica, arnica, arnica!" and the police that were on guard near his room thought he meant anarchy, and they sent four detectives to stay in dad's room.

The people here, the Chicago young man told me, think the Cossacks are human hyenas, that they have had their hearts removed by a surgical operation when young, and a piece of gizzard put in in place of the heart, and that they are natural murderers, the sight of blood acting on them the same as champagne on a human being, and that but for the Cossacks Russia would have a population of loving subjects that would make it safe for the Little Father to go anywhere in Russia unattended, but with Cossacks ready to whip and murder and laugh at suffering, the people are becoming like men bitten by rabid dogs, and they froth at the mouth and have spasms and carry bombs up their sleeves, ready to blow up the members of the royal family, and there you are.

If you do not hear from me after next Sunday you can put dad's obituary and mine in the local papers and say we died of an overdose of Cossack. If we get through this revolution alive you will hear from me, but this is the last revolution I am going to attend.

Yours,

Hennery.

CHAPTER XXI.

St. Petersburg, Russia.—My Dear Grocery-witz: Well, sir, dad and I have got too much of Russia the quickest of any two tourists you ever heard of. That skirmish we saw, the day the Russians blessed the Neva, and shot blank cartridges filled with old iron at the czar, was not a marker to the trouble the next Sunday, when the working people marched to the Winter Palace, to present a petition to the "Little Father."

We thought a revolution was like a play, and that it would be worth going miles to see. Dad was in South America once when there was a revolution, where more than a dozen greasers, with guns that wouldn't shoot, put on a dozen different kinds of uniforms, and yelled: "Down with the government," and frothed at the mouth, and drank buttermilk and yelled Spanish swear words, and acted brave, until a native soldier with white pajamas came out with a gun and shot one of the revolutionists in the thumb, when the revolution was suppressed and the next day the revolutionists were pounding stone, with cannon balls chained to their legs; and dad thought a revolution in Russia would be something like that, and that we could get on a front porch and watch it as it went by, and joke with the revolution, and throw confetti, like it was a carnival, but that Sunday that the Russian revolution was begun, we had enough blood to last us all our lives.

We got a place sitting on an iron picket fence, and we saw the people coming up the street towards the Winter Palace, dressed mostly in blouses, and looking as innocent as a crowd of sewer diggers at home going up to the city hall to ask for a raise in wages of two shillings a day. Nobody had a gun, and no one would have known how to use a gun, and all looked like poor people going to prayers. There were troops everywhere, and every soldier acted as though he was afraid something would happen to spoil their chance of killing anybody. The snow on the streets was clean and as white as the wings of a peace dove, and dad said the show was no better than a parade of laboring men at home on Labor day.

Suddenly some officer yelled to the parade to stop, and the priest at the head of the procession, who was carrying a cross, slowed up a little, like the drum major of a band when the populace at home begins to throw eggs, but they kept on, and then the shooting began, and in a minute men, women and children were rolling in the snow, bleeding and dying, the marchers were too stunned to run, and the deadly guns kept on spitting fire, and the street was full of dead and dying, and then the Cossacks rode over the dead and sabered and knouted the living, and as the snow was patched with red blood, dad fainted away and fell off the picket fence, and hung by one pant leg, which caught on a picket, and crowds rushed in every direction, and it was an hour before I could get a drosky to haul dad to the hotel.

Dad collapsed when he got to the hotel, and I got a doctor and a nurse, and for two days I had to watch the revolution alone, while dad had fits of remorse 'cause he brought me to such a charnel house, he said.

Well, if you ever go anywhere, traveling for pleasure, do not go to Russia, because it is the saddest place on earth. I have seen no person smile or laugh in all the ten days we have been here, except a Cossack when he run a saber through a little girl, and his laugh was like the coyote on the prairie when he captures a little lamb. The people look either heart-broken or snarly, like the people confined in an insane asylum at home.

The czar, who a week ago was loved by the people, who believed if they went to him, as to their God, and appealed for guidance, is to-day hated by all, and instead of "Nicholas the Good," since he scampered away to a castle in the country, and crawled under a bed, all the people call him "the Little Jack Rabbit," and his fate is sealed, as a bomb will blow him into pieces so small they will have to be swept up in a dustpan for burial, maybe before dad and I can get out of Russia.

Going to St. Petersburg for a pleasant outing is a good deal like visiting the Chicago stockyards to watch the bloody men kill the cattle, and the butchers in the stockyards, calloused against any feeling for suffering animals, are like the soldiers here who shoot down their neighbors because they are hired to do so. The murder of those unarmed working men, that Sunday, has changed a helpless, pleading people into anarchists with deadly bombs in their blouses, where they were accustomed to carry black bread to sustain life, and with the menace of Japan in the far east and an outraged people at home, Russia is in a bad way, and if I was the czar or a grand duke, I would find a woodchuck hole and arrange with the woodchuck for a furnished flat.

I didn't think there was going to be anything going on in Russia except bloodshed and bombs, and things to make you sorry that you were here, and I was willing to take chloroform and let them carry me home in a box, with my description on the cover, until the doctor told me that dad was in a condition of nervousness, that he needed something to happen to get his mind off of the awful scenes he had witnessed, and asked me if I couldn't think of something to excite him and wake him up, and then dad said, after he got so he could go out doors: "Hennery, you have always been Johnny on the spot when I needed diversion, and I want you to take your brain apart, and oil the works, and see if you can't conjure up something to get my blood circulating and my pores open for business, and anything you think of goes, and I swear I will not kick if you scare the boots off of me."

Well, that was right into my hand; and I set my mind to strike at four p. m. I had been out riding once with the Chicago man, in a sledge, with three horses abreast, all runaway horses, and the driver was a Cossack who lashed the horses into a run every smooth place he found in the road, and it was like running to a fire, so I got the Chicago fellow to go with me and we found the Cossack, and he was drunker than usual. There is a kind of liquor here called vodka, which skins wood alcohol and carbolic acid to a finish, and when a man is full of it he is so mad he wants to cut his own throat. This driver had put up sideboards on his neck and had two jags in one, and we hired him by the hour.

I told the Chicago man the circumstances and that I had got to get dad out of his trance, and he said he would help me. When I was out riding the day before I noticed that the road was full of great dane dogs, wolf hounds and stag hounds, which followed their master's sledges out in the country, and the dogs loafed around, hungry, looking for bones, and fighting each other, so I decided to get the dogs to chase our sledge and make dad think we were chased by wolves. I thought that would make dad stand without hitching, and it did.

The Chicago man bought some cannon firecrackers, and I bought a cow's liver, and hitched it to a rope, and hid it in the back seat, and my Chicago friend and I took the back seat, and we got dad in the seat behind the driver, and started about an hour before dark out in the country, through a piece of woods that looked quite wolfy. On the way out the driver let his horses run away a few times, like you have seen in Russian pictures, and dad was beginning to sit up and take notice, and seemed to act like a man who expects every minute to be thrown over a precipice and mixed up with dead horses. Dad touched the driver once on the coat-tail and told him not to hurry so confounded fast, and the driver thought he was complaining because it was too slow, and he gave a Comanche yell and threw the lines into the air, and the horses just skedaddled, and run into a snow bank and tipped over the sledge, and piled us out on top of dad, but dad only said: "This is getting good."

We righted up, and dad wanted to know where all the pups came from that we had passed. I had been throwing out pieces of meat into the road for a mile or so, and the dogs were having a picnic. It was getting pretty dark by this time, and we started back to town, and I threw out my liver, fastened to the rope, and the Chicago man, who had given the driver a drink of vodka when we tipped over, told him, in Russian, that when the dogs began to follow us, to get hold of the liver, to yell "wolves," and give the team the rein, for a five-mile run, and yell all the time, because we wanted to give the old gentleman a good time.

Well, uncle, I would have given anything if you could have seen dad, when the dogs began to chase that liver, and bark and fight each other. The driver yelled something in Russian, and pointed back with his whip, the Chicago man said: "My God, we are pursued by a pack of ravenous wolves, and there is no hope for us," and I began to cry, and implored dad, if he loved me, to save me.

Dad stood up in the sledge and looked back, and saw the wolves, and he was scared, but he said the only thing to do was to throw something overboard for them to be chewing on while we got away, but he sat down and pulled a robe over his head and his lips were moving, but I do not know whom he was addressing.

The Chicago man touched off a couple of cannon firecrackers behind the sledge, but that only kept the dogs back for a minute, and dad said probably the best thing to do was to throw me overboard and let them eat me, and I said: "Nay, nay, Pauline," and then I think dad fainted away, for he never peeped again until the team had run away a lot more, and I cut my liver rope, and when we got into the suburbs of St. Petersburg the dogs had overtaken the liver, and were fighting over it.

The driver had to pull up his horses as we struck the town, and dad must have got a whiff of the driver's vodka, because he come to, and we got to the hotel all right, and I thought dad would simply die in his tracks, but the ride and the excitement did him good, and he wanted to buy a gun and go out wolf hunting the next day, but our tickets were bought and we shall get out of this terrible country to-morrow.

Dad woke me, up in the night and wanted to know if I saw him when he pulled his knife and wanted to get out and fight the pack of wolves single-handed. I am not much of a liar, but I told him I remembered it well, and it demonstrated to me that he was as brave a man as the czar, "the Little Jack Rabbit," as his people call him.

Well, thanks to my wolf hunt, dad is all right again, and now we shall go to some country where there is peace. I don't know where we will find it, but if such a country exists, your little Henry will catch on, if dad's money holds out.

Yours, covered with Gore.

Hennery.

CHAPTER XXII.

Constantinople, Turkey.—My Dear Old "Shriner"—We got out of Russia just in time to keep from being arrested or blown up with a bomb. Dad wanted to go to Moscow, because he saw a picture once of Moscow being destroyed by fire by Napoleon, or somebody, and he wanted to see if they had ever built the town up again, but I felt as though something serious was going to, happen in that country if we didn't look out, and so I persuaded dad to go to Turkey, and the day we started for Constantinople we got the news that the Nihilists had thrown a bomb under the carriage of the Grand Duke Sergius and blew him and the carriage into small pieces not bigger than a slice of summer sausage, and they had to sweep his remains up in a dustpan and bury them in a two-quart fruit jar. Wouldn't that jar you?

When dad heard about that you couldn't have kept him in Russia on a bet, and so we let the authorities have all the money we had, giving some to each man who held us up, until we got out of the country, and then we took the first long breath we had taken since we struck the Godforsaken country of the czar. If the bombs hold out I do not think there will be a quorum left in Russia in a year, either czars, dukes or anything except peasants on the verge of starvation and workingmen who have not the heart to work. I wouldn't take the whole of Russia as a gift, and have to dodge bombs night and day.

Say, old man, you never dreamed that I knew all about you and dad joining the Masons that time, but I watched you and dad giving each other signs and grips, and whispering passwords into each other's ears, in the grocery, nights, after you had locked up. I thought, at the time, that you and dad were planning a burglary, but when you both went to the lodge one night and stayed till near morning, and dad came home with a red Turkish fez and told ma that you and he had joined the shrine, which was the highest degree in Masonry, and you and he were nobles, and all that rot, I was on to you bigger than a house, and you couldn't fool me when you and dad winked at each other and talked about crossing the hot sands of the desert.

Well, dad brought his red fez along, 'cause I think he expected he would meet shriners all over the world, that he could borrow money of. When we struck Constantinople and dad saw that every last one of the Turks wore a red fez, he felt as though he had got among shriners, and he got his fez out of his trunk and he wears it all the time.

Dad acts as familiar with the Turks here as though he owned a harem. We go to the low streets, about as wide as a street car, where Turks are selling things, with dad wearing his fez, and he begins to make motions and give grand hailing signs of distress, and the Turks look at him as though he had robbed a bank, and they charge enormous prices for everything, and dad pays with a smile, thinking his brother Masons are fairly giving things away. He looks upon all men who wear the fez as his brothers, and they look at him as though he was crazy in the head.

The only trouble is that dad insists on talking to the women here without an introduction, and a woman in Turkey had rather die than have a Christian dog look at her. Dad was buying some wormy figs of a merchant, who was seated on the floor of his shop, and giving him signs, when a curtain behind the Turk was pulled one side and a woman with beautiful eyes and her face covered with a veil, came out with a cup of coffee for the Turk. Dad shook hands with her, and said: "Your husband and I belong to the same lodge," and he was going to go inside and visit the family, when the woman drew a small dagger out of the folds of her dress, and the Turk drew one of these scimeters, and it looked for a moment as though I was going to be a half orphan, particularly when dad put his hand on her shoulder and petted it, and smiled one of those masher smiles which he uses at home, and said: "My good woman, you must not get in the habit of jabbing your husband's friends with this crooked cutlery, though to be killed by so handsome a woman would indeed be a sweet death," but the bluff did not go, and the woman disappeared behind the curtain, and dad had the frantic husband to deal with.

When Dad Put his Hand on Her Shoulder and Petted It 276

I have never seen a human being look as murderous as that Turk did as he drew his thumb across the blade of his knife, drew up his lip and snarled like a dog that has been bereaved of a promising bone by a brother dog that was larger.

The Turk looked through his teeth, and his eyes seemed to act like small arc lights, that were to show him where to cut dad, and dad began to turn pale, and looked scared.

"Give him the grand hailing sign of distress," said I as dad leaned against a barrel of dried prunes. Dad said he had forgotten the sign, and then I told him the only way out of it, alive, would be to buy something, so dad picked up a little jim-crack worth about ten cents, and gave the Turk a five-dollar gold piece, and while the Turk went in behind the curtain to get the change I told dad now was the time to skip, and you ought to have seen dad make a sprint out the door and around a corner, and up another street, while I followed him, and we got away from the danger of being stabbed, but dad got his foot into it again before we had gone a block.

Nobody in Constantinople ever hurries, or goes off a walk, so when the people saw an old man, with a fez on his head, running amuck, as they say here, followed by a beautiful boy, they began to crawl into their holes, thinking dad was crazy, but when we were passing a sausage store, where about 20 dogs were asleep in the street, and dad kicked half a dozen dogs and yelled, "get out, you hounds," that settled it, and they knew he was wrong in the head, and they yelled for the police, and we were pulled for fast driving, and taken before a Turkish justice of the peace, followed by the whole crowd.

Get out You Hounds 282

The justice did not wear a fez, but had on a turban, so dad did not give him any signs, but after jabbering a while they sent for an interpreter, who could talk pigeon English, and then dad had a trial, and I acted as his lawyer. I told about how dad had tried to be kind and genial to another man's wife, and how, in his hurry to get away from the murderous husband he fell over a mess of dogs, and that he was a distinguished American, who was in Turkey to negotiate a loan to the sultan.

Say, that fixed them, and they all made salams to dad, and bowed all over themselves, and the justice of the peace prayed to Allah, and the interpreter said we could go, but to be careful about touching a Turkish woman or a dog, particularly a dog, as the Turks were very sensitive on the dog question. So we went out of the courtroom and wandered around the town, and you can bet that dad didn't look at any more women, though they were everywhere with veils that covered their faces so nothing but their eyes could be seen.

Gee, but you never saw such eyes as these Turkish women have. They are big and black, and they go right through you, and clinch on the other side. Dad says the facilities for getting into trouble are better in Constantinople than any place we have been, as the men look like bandits and the women look like executioners. Dad thanked me for helping him out of that scrape by claiming he was the agent of a financial syndicate that wanted to lend money to the sultan. If I had said dad was a collecting agency, to make the sultan pay up, they would have sentenced him to be boiled in oil.

Well, we thought we had been in trouble before, but we are in it now worse than ever. We heard at the hotel that at 11 o'clock in the morning the sultan would pass by in a carriage, with an escort, on the way to a mosque, to pray to Allah, and everybody could see the sultan, so we got a place on a balcony, and at the appointed time the procession came in sight. It was imposing, but solemn, and the people on both sides of the street acted like they do in America when the funeral of a great man is passing. No man spoke, and all looked as though they expected, if they moved, to be arrested and have a stone tied to their feet and thrown into the Bosphorus, the way they kill one of the sultan's wives when she flirts with a stranger.

We watched the soldiers, and finally the carriage of the sultan came, and in it was a dried up man, with liver complaint, with a nose like an eagle, and eyes like shoe buttons. He looked as though death would be a relief, and yet he seemed afraid of it, and there was no sound of welcome, such as there would be if Roosevelt was riding down Michigan avenue at Chicago, on the way to the stockyards to pray to Armour, instead of to Allah.

You could have heard a pin drop. I said: "Dad, this is too solemn, even for a sultan. Let's give him the university yell, and show that mummy that he has got two friends in Constantinople, anyway." "Here she goes," says dad, and we leaned over the railing, just as the sultan's carriage was right in front of us and not ten feet away, and in that oppressive silence dad and I opened up, "U-Rah-Rah-Wis-Con-Sin, zip-boom-Ah!" and then we started to sing, "There'll Be a Hot Time in the Old Town To-Night."

There'll Be a Hot Time in the Old Town To-night 279

Well, if any man in the crowd had touched off a bomb, there could have been no greater consternation. The sultan turned pale, as pale as so yellow a man could, and became faint, and fell over into the arms of a general who sat beside him, the Bazi Bazouks on horseback began to ride up and down the street, the crowd scattered, the sultan's carriage was turned around and rushed back to the palace, with the ruler of Turkey having a fit, and about a hundred soldiers came up on the veranda, where dad and I had broke up the procession, and they lit on dad like buzzards on a dead horse, and took possession of the hotel, and began to search our baggage.

Another Took Me by the Ear 285

One Turk choked dad until his tongue hung out of his mouth, and another took me by the ear and stretched it out so it was long as a mule's ear, and they took us to a bastile and dad says it is all up with us now, because they will drown us like a mess of kittens in a bag, and all because we woke them up with a football yell in the wrong place.

Well, we might as well wind up our career here as anywhere. Good-by, old man. You will see our obituary in the papers.

Your repentant,

Hennery.

CHAPTER XXIII.

Constantinople, Turkey.—My Dear Grocer-pasha: When I wrote you last I thought you would be in mourning for dad and I before this, as there seemed nothing for the Turks to do but to kill us after we had stampeded the sultan and all his soldiers by giving them a university yell, but after we had been confined in a sort of jail over night, dad and I had a heart to heart talk, and my diplomacy saved us for the time being. I told dad that what we wanted to do was to tell the Turks that dad represented the American people, and had a communication to make to the sultan personally, which would make him rich and happy.

Well, say, they bit like a bass, and the next day they took us before the sultan at the palace. Dad dug up a package of blank gold mining stock in a mine that he was going to promote, though the mine was only a small hole in the ground, and the stock had been offered for one cent a share, the par value being a hundred dollars, so a man who got a share for a cent would, when the mine got to paying, get a hundred dollars for every cent he invested.

Dad filled out one of the stock certificates for 1,000,000 shares, which would represent a capital equal to all the debts of Turkey, and we went before the sultan, and we couldn't have been treated better if we had owned a brewery. Dad told his story to the sultan through an interpreter, while I looked around at the gorgeous surroundings and tried to think of something to do to wake them up.

Dad said he came right fresh from the American people, and was authorized by his mining company to present the sultan with untold millions, for pure love of the Turkish people, whom they had seen riding and leading camels at the Chicago world's fair, and dad produced the stock certificate for 1,000,000 shares of stock in the Golden Horn Gold Mining and Smelting company, and took out a handful of $20 gold pieces and showed them to the crowd as specimens of gold that came from our mine.

He said our people did not expect anything in return, but just desired the good will of the Turkish empire. He said that President Roosevelt desired him to present his warmest regards to the sultan, and to invite him to visit America, and if he would consent to do so, an American war vessel would be furnished for him and the white house would be turned over to him for his harem, and dad said the president wanted him particularly to impress upon the sultan that if he came he must bring his folks, all his wives that would be apt to size up for beauty with our American women.

He Must Bring his Folks, and All His Wives 289

Well, you ought to have seen that sickly looking sultan brace up when dad handed him the millions of mining stock, and he grabbed the paper like an old clothes buyer would grab a dress suit that a wife had sold for 60 cents, belonging to her husband. He also wanted to see the gold that dad had shown as coming from the mine, and when dad showed him the yellow boys he took them as souvenirs and put them in his girdle, and then I thought dad would faint, but he kept his nerve like a poker player betting on a bobtail flush.

The sultan asked so many questions about America that I was afraid dad would get all balled up, but he kept his nerve, and lied as though he was on the witness stand trying to save his life. Dad told the sultan he was authorized by the American people to inquire into the industries of Turkey, and what he particularly desired was an insight into the harems, as a national institution, because many American people were gradually adopting the customs of the orient, and he desired to report to congress as to whether we should adopt the customs of Turkey with her dried prunes and dates with worms in, and her attar of roses made of pig's lard; her fez, to cure baldness, and her outlandish pants and peaked red Morocco shoes, and her harems.

The sultan said he would like to show us a little bunch of the cream of the harem, who would do a stunt in the way of dancing, to celebrate the good feeling of the American people, and the visit of the distinguished statesman and gold miner to his realm, and dad said the sultan couldn't turn his stomach with no cream of the harem, only they must keep their hands off him, and the sultan promised he should be as safe as a "unique," whatever that is.

Dad and I had hired knee breeches and things of a masquerade ball store, and we didn't look half bad when the crowd of shieks and things formed a crescent around the sultan, who sat in a sort of barber's chair with an awning over it, and they sounded a hewgag or something, and about a dozen pretty fine looking females, dressed like the ballet in a vaudeville show, came in and began to dance before the sultan.

Dad stood it first rate until a girl got on the carpet barefooted and began one of those willowy sort of dances that nearly broke up the Chicago fair, when people left the buildings filled with the work of the world's artists, in all lines of progress, and went to the Midway in a body to see "Little Egypt," but when this dancer waltzed up to dad and wiggled in a foreign language, dad sashayed up to her and I couldn't hold him back.

He Was Just Getting Warmed up

He was just getting warmed up to "balance to partners," when a frown came over the sultan's face and he looked cross at dad, and then the hewgag sounded, and the girls scattered out of a side door and dad wanted to follow, but I held him by the coat, and it was over. I think those girls were the only ones in the whole harem that were good looking.

Dad breathed hard a little from his exercise, and said he was ready to inspect the stock, and the sultan detailed a tall negro, with a face dried up like a mummy, and we started out through the harem, dad pulling the long hair on the side of his head over his bald spot, and throwing his shoulders back and drawing in his stomach to make him look young.

Well, say, there is nothing about a harem, much different from keeping house at home, except that there is more of it. The idea people get of harems is that the women are all young and beautiful, and that they sit around a swimming tank and play guitars and keep the flies off the man who owns the place, while he smokes the vile Turkish tobacco burning in a jardiniere, through a section of rubber hose, and goes to sleep like a Chinaman smoking opium, and that they drink rare wines and dance with bangles on their legs and ropes of pearls on their necks and arms.

I have seen alleged imitations of a Turkish harem on the stage, with American girls doing the acting, and it would make you feel as though you would invest in a harem when you got old enough, but, gee, when you see a regular harem, run by an up-to-date Turk, you think of the Mormon apostle who has 40 wives of all ages, from 70 down to a 16-year-old hired girl, with a hair-lip and warts on her thumbs. This harem was like a big stock barn in the states, with a big room to exercise the colts, and box stalls for the different wives and their families to live in and do their own cooking and washing.

   Instead of sitting by a bath playing a harp, the poor old wives stand by a washtub and play tunes on the washboard, and scrub, and take care of children. I thought the custom of spanking children was an American institution, but it is as old as the ages, for I saw a Turkish mother grab up a child that had lifted a kitten by the tail, and take it across her knee and give it a few with a red hand covered with soapsuds, and the young Turk yelled bloody murder, just like an American kid, and then sat down on its knees, so the spanking wouldn't hurt, and called its mother names in a language I couldn't understand, but I knew what the child said, by instinct. Dad started to interfere, because he is a member of the humane society, but the unique that was showing us around saved dad's life by pushing him along, before the woman got a chance to brain him with the washboard.

   The women mostly had on these baggy Turkish trousers, like the Zouaves wear, and a jacket, and a cloth around their heads, and they acted as though if the next meal came along all right they would be in luck. We saw a few women pretty white, and they were Circassian slaves, with big eyes and hoops in their ears, and a little different clothes on, but there were none that dad would buy at an auction, or at a bargain sale, if they were marked down to 99 cents.

   We passed one woman running an American sewing machine, and dad said he'd bet she was an American, and he went up to her and said: "Hello, sis!" She stopped the machine, looked up at dad with a sort of Bowery expression, and said: "Gwan, Chauncey Depew, you old peach, or I'll have you pinched," and the unique took dad by the arm and pulled him along real spry, but he hung back and looked over his shoulder at the woman, but she went on sewing, and dad said to me: "Well, wouldn't that frost you?" And we went on making the inspection.

   I don't think I ever saw so many children, outside of an orphan asylum, all about the same size and all looking exactly alike. They all had the same beady black eyes that look as though they were afraid of getting caught in a trap, like muskrats, and their noses had the same inquiring appearance, as though the owner was speculating as to how much money the visitors had in their pockets, and whether it was fastened in. Race suicide is impossible in Turkey, but a race of bandits is growing up that will let no foreigners with a pocketbook escape.

   It took us an hour to go through the harem, and it was more like going through the quarters of the working women of a home laundry in the tenement district of a large city, than a comic opera, as we had been led to expect by what we had read of harems. When we went into the harem I think dad was going to insist on having the women dance for him, while he sat on a throne and threw kisses at the most beautiful women in all the world, but before we had got around all the box stalls I think if any of them had started to dance dad would have stampeded in a body.

   We finally got back to the great marble room, where the sultan was sleeping in a stuffed chair, surrounded by his staff, and one of them woke him up, and he asked dad what he thought of the home life of a crowned head, and dad said it beat anything he had ever seen, and he should recommend to his government that the harem system be adopted in America, and actually the sultan seemed pleased. He said as an evidence of his love for America he wanted to present to the president, through dad, 50 of his wives, and if dad would indicate where he wanted them delivered, they would be there, Johnny on the spot, or words to that effect.

At first I thought dad would faint away, but I whispered to him that it would be discourteous to decline a present, after giving the sultan a gold mine, and that may be the old man would be so mad, if he declined the wives, that he would tie stones to our legs and sink us in the Bosphor-ous, so dad rallied and said, on behalf of his government, he would accept the kindly and thoughtful gift of his highness, and that he would cable for a war vessel to take the wives to his own America, and he would notify the sultan when to round them up and load them on the vessel.

Well, sir, I do not know what possessed me to make a scene, before we got out of the presence of the sultan, but it all came to me sudden, like an inspiration comes to a poet. I had been eating some fruit that I bought in a paper bag, and when I had eaten the last of it, I wondered what I would do with the bag, and then I thought what fun it would be to blow the bag up, and suddenly burst it, when all was still. So I blowed up the bag, so it was as hard as a bladder, and tied a string around the neck, and waited. I did not think how afraid everybody in these old countries is of bombs, or I never would have done it, honestly.

The sultan was signing some papers, and looking out of the corners of his eyes to see if anybody was present who was suspicious, and dad was getting ready to make a salam, and back out of the presence of the ruler of Turkey, when I got behind some of the officials who were watching the sultan, and I laid my paper bag on the marble floor, and it was as still as death, and all you could hear was the scratching of the pen, when I jumped up in the air as though I had a fit, and yelled "Allah," and came down with my whole weight on the paper bag, and of all the stampedes you ever saw, that was the worst.

Stampede 299

You know what a noise it makes to bust a paper bag. Well, this was the toughest old bag I ever busted, and it sounded like a cannon fired down cellar somewhere, and the air was full of dust, and before I could get up the sultan had tipped over the table and run yelling into another room, praying to "Allah," and all the staff had lit out for tall timber, and there was nobody left but dad and the unique and myself, and the unique took dad by the arm and started for the door, and we were fired out.

As I went out of the room I looked around, and there was a Turk's head sticking out of every door to see how many had been killed by the bomb, and as we got out doors, dad said "Now we have to get out of Turkey before night, or we die. Me for Egypt, boy, if we can catch a boat before we are drawn and quartered." So here goes for Cairo, Egypt.

Yours only,
Hennery.

CHAPTER XXIV.

Cairo, Egypt.—My Dear Old Irish Vegetable: Gee, but you ought to see dad and I right now at a hotel, waiting for a chance at a room, when a bride and groom get ready to vacate it, and go somewhere else. This hotel is full of married people who look scared whenever there is a new arrival, and I came pretty near creating a panic by going into the parlor of the hotel, where a dozen couples were sitting around making goo-goo eyes at each other, and getting behind a screen and, in a disguised voice, shouting, "I know all! Prepare to defend yourself!"

The women turned pale and some said, "At last! At last!" while others got faint in the head, and some fell on the bosoms of their husbands and said: "Don't shoot!" You see, most of these wives had husbands somewhere else that might be looking for them. I have warned dad not to be seen conversing with a woman, or he may be shot by a husband who is on her trail, or by the husband she has with her.

Well, sir, of all the trips we have had anywhere, the trip from Constantinople here was the limit. For two or three days we were on dinky steamboats with Arabs, Turks, negroes and all nationalities camping on deck, full of fleas, and with cholera germs on them big enough to pick like blueberries, and all of the passengers were dirty and eat things that would make a dog in America go mad. The dog biscuit that are fed to American dogs would pass as a delicate confection on the menu of any steamboat we struck, and I had rather lie down in a barn yard with a wet dog for a pillow and a cast-off blanket from a smallpox hospital for a bed, than to occupy the bridal chamber of any steamboat we struck.

And then the ride across the desert by rail to reach Cairo was the worst in the world. Passengers in rags, going to Mecca, or some other place of worship, eating cheese a thousand years old made from old goat's milk, and dug from the Pyramids too late to save it, was what surrounded us, and the sand storm blew through the cars laden with germs of the plague, and stuck to us so tight you couldn't get it off with sandpaper, and when we got here all we have had to do is to bathe the dirt off in layers.

It Takes Nine Baths to Get Down To American Epidermis 304

It takes nine baths to get down to American epidermis, and the last bath has a jackplane to go with it, and a thing they scale fish with. But we are all right now, with rooms in the hotel, and rested, and when we go home we are going to be salted down and given chloroform and shipped as mummies. Dad insists that he will never cross a desert or an ocean again, and I don't know what is to become of us. Anyway, we are going to enjoy ourselves until we are killed off.

The first two days we just looked about Cairo, and saw the congress of nations, for there is nothing just like this town anywhere. There are people from all quarters of the globe, the most outlandish and the most up-to-date. This place is an asylum for fakirs and robbers, a place where defaulters, bribers, murderers, swindlers and elopers are safe, as there seems to be no extradition treaty that cannot be overcome by paying money to the officials. I found that out the first day, and told dad we should have no standing in the society of Egypt unless the people thought he had committed some gigantic crime and fled his country.

Dad wanted to know how it would strike me if it was noised about the hotel that he had robbed a national bank, but I, told him there would be nothing uncommon or noticeable about robbing a bank, as half the tourists were bank defaulters, so he would have to be accused of something startling, so we decided that dad should be charged with being the principal thing in the Standard Oil Company, and that he had underground pipe lines running under several states, gathering oil away from the people who owned it, and that at the present time he was worth a billion dollars, and his income was $9,000,000 every little while, and, by ginger, you ought to see the people bow down to him. Say, common bank robbers and defaulters just fell over themselves to get acquainted with dad, and to carry out the joke, I put some kerosene oil on dad's handkerchief, and that clinched it, for everybody loves the smell of a perfume that represents a billion dollars.

All the women wanted to dance with dad in the hotel dance, and because they thought I must be heir to all the oil billions, they wanted to hold me on their laps, and stroke my hair, as though I was it. I guess we are going to have everything our own way here, and if dad does not get eloped with by some Egyptian princess, I shall be mistaken. The Egyptians are pretty near being negroes, and wear bangles in their ears, and earrings on their arms. You take it in the dark, and let a princess put her arms around you, and sort of squeeze you, and you can't tell but what she is white, only there is an odor about them like "Araby the blessed," but in the light they are only negroes, a little bleached, with red paint on their cheeks. If I was going to marry an Egyptian woman, I would take her to Norway, or up towards the north pole, where it is night all day, and you wouldn't realize that you were married to a colored woman. To be around among these Egyptians is a good deal like having a pass behind the scenes at the play of Ben Hur in New York, only here the dark and dangerous women are the real thing, instead of being white girls with black paint on.

We have just got back from the pyramids, and dad is being treated for spinal meningitis, on account of riding a camel. I never tried harder to get dad to go anywhere on the cars than I did to get him to go to the pyramids by rail, as a millionaire should, but he said he was going to break a camel to the saddle, and then buy him and take him home for a side show. So we went down to the camel garage and hired a camel for dad, and four camels for the arabs and things he wanted for an escort, and a jackass for me. There were automobiles and carriages, and trolleys, and everything that we could have hired, and been comfortable for the ten-mile ride, but dad was mashed on the camel, and he got it.

Well, sir, it was not one of these world's fair camels that lay down for you to get on, and then got up on the installment plan, and chuck you forward and aft, but a proud Egyptian camel that stands up straight and makes you climb up on a stepladder.

Dad got along up the camel's ribs, when the-stepladder fell, and he grabbed hold of the hair on the two humps, and the humps were loose and they lopped over on the side, and it must have hurt the camel's feelings to have his humps pulled down, so he reached around his head and took a mouthful out of the seat of dad's pants, and dad yelled to the camel to let go, and the Arabs amputated the camel from dad's trousers, and pushed dad up on top with a bamboo pole with a crotch in it, and when dad got settled between the humps he said, "Let 'er go," and we started.

Dad could have had a camel with a platform on top, and an awning, but he insisted on taking his camel raw, and he sat there between those humps, his trousers worked up towards his knees, showing his red socks and blue drawers, and his face got pale from sea sickness, and the red, white and blue colors made me think of a fourth of July at home. We went out of town like a wild west show, and dad seemed happy, except that every time an automobile went whizzing along, dad's camel got the jumps and waltzed sideways out into the sandy desert, and chewed at dad's socks, so part of the time dad had to draw up his legs and sit on one hump and put his shoes on the other hump. The Arabs on the other camels would ride up alongside and steer dad's camel back into the road, by sticking sharp sticks into the camel, and the animal would yawn and groan and make up faces at me on my jackass, and finally dad wanted to change works with me and ride my jackass, but I told him we had left the stepladder back at Cairo, so dad hung to his mountainous steed, but the dust blew so you couldn't see, and it was getting monotonous when the queerest thing happened.

You have heard that camels can fill up with water and go for a week without asking for any more. Well, I guess the week was up, and it was time to load the camels with water, for as we came to the Nile every last camel made a rush for the river, and they went in like a yoke of oxen on a stampede, and waded in clear up to the humps, and began to drink, and dad yelled for a life preserver and pulled his feet up on top and sat there like a frog on a pond lily leaf.

Sat There Like a Frog on A Pond Lily Leaf 308

My jackass only stepped his feet in the edge, and dad wanted me to swim my jackass out to the camel and let him fall off onto the jack, but I knew dad would sink my jack in a minute, and I wouldn't go in the river. Well, the camels drank about an hour, with dad sitting there meditating, and then the dragomen got them out, and we started off for the pyramids, which were in plain sight like the pictures you have seen, with palm trees along the Nile, and Arabs camping on the bank, and it looked as though everything was going to be all right, when suddenly dad's camel stopped dead still and wouldn't move a foot, and all the rest of the camels stopped, closed their eyes and went to sleep, and the Arabs went to sleep, and dad and the jackass and I were apparently the only animals in Egypt that were awake.

Dad kicked his camel in the ribs, but it wouldn't budge. He asked me if I could't think up some way to start the procession, and I stopped my jackass and thought a minute, and told dad I had it. I had bought some giant fire crackers and roman candles at Cairo, with which I was going to fire a salute on top of the biggest pyramid, to celebrate for old America, and I told dad what I had got, and I thought if I got off my jackass and fired a salute there in the desert it would wake them up.

Dad said, "all right, let 'er go, but do it sort of easy, at first, so not to overdo it," and I got my artillery ready. Say, you can't fire off fireworks easy, you got to touch a match to 'em and dodge and take your chances. Well, I scratched a match and lit the giant fire cracker, and put it under the hind legs of dad's camel, and when it got to fizzing I lit my roman candle, and as the fire cracker exploded like a 16-inch gun, my roman candle began to spout balls of fire, and I aimed one at each camel, and the whole push started on a stampede for the pyramids, the camels groaning, the Arabs praying to Allah, dad yelling to stop 'er, and my jackass led the bunch, and I was left in the desert to pick up the hats.

I guess I will have to tell you' the rest of the tragedy in my next letter.

Yours with plenty of sand,

Hennery.

CHAPTER XXV.

Cairo, Egypt.—My Dear Old Geezer: I broke off my last letter in sight of the pyramids, when I was left alone on the desert, my jackass having stampeded with the camels, on account of my fireworks, and I presume you think I was all in, but I got to the pyramids before the stampeded caravan did. I saw a car coming along, and I just got aboard and in ten minutes I was at the base of the big pyramid, and the camel with dad on between the humps, was humping himself half a mile away, trying to get there, and the other camels, with the Arabs, were stretched out like horses in a race, behind, and my jackass was right next to dad's camel, braying and occasionally kicking dad's camel in the slats.

There were about a hundred tourists around the stampede of the camels, and I told them my the base of the big pyramid, all looking towards dad, the great American millionaire, was on the runaway camel in advance, and asked them to form a line across the trail and save dad, but when the camel came nearer I was ashamed of dad. He had his arms around the front hump of the camel, and he was yelling for help to stop his menagerie, and his legs were flying in the air, and every time they came down they kicked a hole in the side of the camel.

Well, sir, I thought dad was a brave man, but he blatted like a calf, and when the camel stopped and went to eating a clump of grass dad opened his eyes, and when he saw that the procession had stopped he rolled off his camel like a bag of wheat, and stuck in the sand and began to say a prayer, but when he saw me standing there, laughing, he stopped praying, and said to me: "I thought you were blown up when that jackass kicked the can of dynamite. You have more lives than a cat. Now, get a hustle on you and we will climb that pyramid, and then quit this blasted country," and dad sat down on a hummock and began to pull himself together, after the most fearful ride he ever had. He said the camel loped, trotted, galloped, single-footed and shied all at the same time, and when one hump was not jamming him in the back the other hump was kicking him in the stomach, and if he had a gun he would shoot the camel, and the Arabs, and bust up the show.

By the time dad got so he could stand up without leaning against a pyramid the Arabs came up and they all talked at once, and drew knives, and it seemed as though they were blaming dad for something. We found an interpreter among the tourists, and he talked with the Arabs, and pointing to the camel dad had ridden, which was stretched out on the sand like he was dead, he told dad the Arabs wanted him to pay for the camel he had ridden to death, and foundered by letting it drink a wagon load of water, and then entered in a race across the desert, and the interpreter said dad better pay, or they would kill him.

Dad settled for the camel for a hundred dollars, and a promise of the skin of the camel, which he was going to take home and have stuffed. Then a man who pretended to be a justice of the peace had dad arrested for driving off of a walk, and he was fined $10 and costs for that, and then all the Arabs stuck him for money for one thing and another, and when he had settled all around and paid extra for not riding back to Cairo on the camel, we got ready to climb up the pyramid. Dad said he wouldn't ride that camel back to Cairo for a million dollars, for he was split up so his legs began where his arms left off, and he was lame from Genesis to Revelations.

But I never saw such a lot of people to pray as these pirates are. Just before they rob a man they get down on their knees on a rug, and mumble something to some god, and after they have got you robbed good and plenty, they get down and pray while they are concealing the money they took from you. Gee, but when I get home I am going to steer the train robbers and burglars onto the idea of always being on praying grounds.

Well, I told dad he hadn't better try to climb up the pyramid, that I would go up, 'cause I could climb like a goat, and when I got up to the top I would fire a salute, so everybody would know that a star spangled American was on deck, but dad said he would go up or quit the tourist business. He said he had come thousands of miles to climb the pyramids, and sit in the shadow of the spinks, and by ginger he was going to do it, and so we started.

Well, say, each stone is about four feet high, and dad couldn't get up without help, so an Arab would go up a stone ahead, and take hold of dad's hands, and two more Arabs would get their shoulders under dad's pants, and shove, and he would get up gradually. We got about half way up when dad weakened, and said he didn't care so much about pyramids as he thought he did, and he was ready to quit, but the guide and some of the tourists said we were right near the entrance to the great tomb of the kings, and that we better go in and at least make a formal call on the crowned heads, and so we went in, through dark passages, with little candles that the guides carried, and up and down stairs, until finally we got into a big room that smelled like a morgue, with bats and evil looking things all around, and I felt creepy.

The guides got down on their knees to pray, and I thought it was time to be robbed again. I do not know what made me think of making a sensation right there in the bowels of that pyramid, where there were corpses thousands of years old, of Egypt's rulers. I never felt that way at home, when I visited a cemetery, but I though I would shoot my last roman candle and fire my last giant firecracker right there in that moseleum, and take the chances that we would get out alive. So when the tourists were lined up beside a tomb of some Rameses or other, and the guides were praying for strength and endurance, probably, to get away with all the money we had, I picked out a place up toward the roof that seemed full of bats and birds of ill omen, and I sneaked my roman candle out from under my shirt, and touched the fuse to a candle on the turban of a guide who was on his knees, and just as the first fire ball was ready to come out I yelled "Whoop-la-much-a wano, epluribus un-um," and the fire balls lighted up the gloom and knocked the bats gaily west.

Holy jumping cats, but you ought to have seen the guides, yelling Allah! Allah! and groveling on the floor, and the bats were flying around in the faces of the tourists, and everybody was simply scared out of their boots. I thought I might as well wind the thing up glorious, so I touched the tail of my last giant firecracker to the sparks that were oozing out of my empty roman candle, and threw it into the middle of the great room, and when it went off you would think a cannon had exploded, and everybody rushed for the door, and we fell over each other getting out through the passage towards the door.

I was the first to get out on to the side of the pyramid, and I watched for the crowd to come out. The tourists got out first, and then dad came out, puffing and wheezing, and the last to come out were the Arabs, and they came on their hands and knees, calling to Mr. Allah and every one of them actually pale, and I think they were conscience-stricken, for they began to give back the money they had robbed dad of, and an Arab must be pretty scared to give up any of his hard-earned robberies. I think dad was about the maddest man there was, until he got some of his money back, when he felt better, but he gave me a talking to that I will never forget.

He said: "Don't you know better than to go around with explosives, like a train robber, and fire them off in a hole in the ground, where there is no ventilation, and make people's ears ring? Maybe you have woke up those kings and queens in there, and changed a dynasty, you little idiot." The rest of the crowd wanted to throw me down the side of the pyramid, but I got away from them and went up on top of the pyramid and hoisted a small American flag, and left it floating there, and then came back to where the crowd was discussing the explosion in the tomb, and then we all went down the side of the pyramid.

The guides got their nerve back after they got out in the air, because they wouldn't help dad down unless he paid them something every stone they helped him climb down, so when he got down he didn't have any money, and hardly any pants, because what pants the Arabs didn't tear were worn off on the stones, so when he showed up in front of the spinks he was a sight, and he bought a turban of a guide and unwound it and wound it around him in place of pants. I was ashamed of dad myself, and it is pretty hard to make me ashamed.

We went back to Cairo on the cars, and what do you think, that dead camel that the Arabs made dad pay for was with the caravan going back to town, 'cause we saw him out of the car window with the hair wore off where dad kicked him in the side. The tourists say the Arabs have that camel trained to die every day when they get to the pyramids, and they make some tenderfoot pay for him at the end of each journey. Dad is going to try to get his money back from the Egyptian government, but I guess he will never realize on his claim.

Well, sir, after dad had doctored all night to get the camel rheumatism and spinal meningitis out of his system, we took a trip by boat on the Nile, and saw the banks where the people grow crops by irrigation, and where an English syndicate has built a big dam, so the whole valley can be irrigated, and I tell you it will not be long before Egypt will raise everything used in the world on that desert, and every other country that raises food to sell will be busted up in business, but it is disgusting to take a trip on the Nile, 'cause all the natives are dirty and sick with contagious diseases, and they are lazy and crippled, and beg for a living, and if you don't give them something they steal all you got. You are in luck if you get away without having leprosy, or the plague, or cholera, or fleas.

So we went back to Cairo, and there was the worst commotion you ever saw, about my fireworks in the tomb. The papers said that an American dynamiter had attempted to blow up the great pyramid, and take possession of the country and place it under the American flag, and that the conspirators were spotted and would be arrested and put in irons as soon as they got back from a trip on the Nile.

Well, sir, dad found his career would close right here, and that he would probably spend the balance of his life in an Egyptian prison if we didn't get out, so we made a sneak and got into our hotel, bought disguises and are going to get out of here tonight, and try to get to Gibraltar, or somewhere in sight of home. Dad is disguised as a shiek, with whiskers and a white robe, like a bath robe, and I am going to travel with him as an Egyptian girl till we get through the Suez canal.

Gee, but I wouldn't be a nigger girl only to save dad.

Your innocent,

Hennery.

CHAPTER XXVI.

Gibraltar, in Spain and England. My Dear Foster Uncle: It seems good to get somewhere that you can hear the English language spoken by the Irish, and the English soldiers are nearly all Irish. When you think of the way the British government treats the Irish, and then you look on while an orderly sergeant calls the roll of a company, and find that nine out of ten answer to Irish names, and only one out of ten has the cockney accent, you feel that the Irish ought to rule England, and an O'Rourke or a O'Shaunnessy should take the place of King Edward. It makes a boy who was brought up in an Irish ward in America feel like he was at home to mix with British soldiers who come from the old sod. Dad says that there is never an army anywhere in the world, except the armies of Russia and Japan, that the bravest men are not answering to Irish names, and always on the advance in a fight, or in the rear when there is a retreat. Dad says that in our own army, when the North and South were fighting, the Irish boys were the fellows who saved the day. They wanted to fight nights and Sundays, and never struck for an eight-hour day, or union wages. When the fighting was over, and soldiers were sick, or discouraged, and despondent, an Irish soldier would come along, maybe on crutches, or with a bullet in his inwards, and tell funny stories and make the discouraged fellows laugh in spite of themselves, and when another fight was on, you had to tie the wounded Irish soldiers to their cots in the hospital, or put them in jail to keep them from forgetting their wounds, and going to the front for one more fight. Dad says if there was an Irish nation with an army and navy, the whole world would have to combine to whip them, and yet the nation that has the control of the Irish people treats them worse than San Francisco treats Chinamen, makes them live on potatoes, and allows landlords to take away the potatoes if they are shy on the rent. Gosh, if I was an Irishman I would see the country that walked on my neck in hell before I would fight for it. (Gee, dad looked over my shoulder and saw what I had written, and he cuffed me on the side of the head, and said I was an incendiary and that I ought to have sense enough not to write treason while a guest on British soil.) Well, I don't care a darn. It makes me hot under the collar when I think of the brave Irish fellows, and I wonder why they don't come to America in a body and be aldermen and policemen. When I get home I am going to join the Fenians, and raise thunder, just as quick as I am old enough.

Keep Away from the Banks for Fear The Banks Will Cave In 329

Well, sir, we have been through the Suez canal, and for a great modern piece of engineering it doesn't size up with a sewer in Milwaukee, or a bayou in Louisiana. It is just digging a railroad cut through the desert, and letting in the water, and there you are. The only question in its construction was plenty of dredging machines, and a place to pile the dirt, and water that just came in of its own accord, and stays there, and smells like thunder, and you see the natives look at it, and keep away from the banks for fear the banks will cave in on them, and give them a bath before their year is up, cause they don't bathe but once a year, and when they skip a year nobody knows about it, except that they smell a year or so more frowsy, like butter that has been left out of the ice box. Our boat went right along, and got out of the canal, because it was a mail boat, but the most of the boats we saw were tied up to the bank, waiting for the millennium. We saw some Russian boats waiting for the war to blow over and as we passed them every Russian on board looked scared, as though we were Japs that were going to fire a torpedo under them, or throw a bomb on deck, and when our boat got by the Russian boat, the crew was called to prayers, to thank the Lord, or whoever it is that the Russians thank, because they had escaped a dire peril. I guess the Russians are all in, and that those who have not gone to the front are shaking hands with themselves, and waiting for the dove of peace to alight on their guns. The Suez canal probably pays, and no wonder, cause they charge what they please to boats that go through, and if they don't pay all they have to do is to stay out, and go around a few thousand miles. It is like a ferry across a little stream out west, where there is no other way to cross, except to wade or go around, and the old ferryman sizes up the wagon load that wants to cross, and takes all they have got loose, and then the travelers are ahead of the game, cause if they didn't cross the stream they would have to camp on the bank until the stream dried up. Some day an earthquake will split that desert wide open and the water in the Suez canal will soak into the sand and the steamboats will lay in the mud, and be covered with a sand storm, and future ages will be discovering full rigged ships down deep on the desert. Dad says we better sell our stock in the canal and buy air ship stock. And talk about business, there is more tonnage goes through the Soo canal, between Michigan and Canada than goes through the Suez and we don't howl about it very much.

Well, sir, I have studied Gibraltar in my geography, and read about it in the papers, and seen its pictures in advertisements, but never realized what a big thing it was. Now, who ever thought of putting that enormous rock right there on that prairie, but God. I suppose the English, when they saw that rock, thought the good Lord had put it there for the English to drill holes in, for guns, and when the Lord was busy somewhere else, the English smoughed the rock away from Spain, by playing a game with loaded dice, and when England got it, that country decided to arm it like a train robber, and hold up the other nations of the earth. When a vessel passes that rock it has to hold up its hands and salute the British flag, or get a mess of hardware fired into its vital parts, but that is all it amounts to, cause it couldn't win any battle for England, and could only sink trading vessels. The walls of the rock are perforated from top to bottom, with holes big enough for guns to squirt smoke and shells, but if the enemy should stay away from right in front of the holes, they might shoot till doomsday and never hit anything but fishing smacks and peddlers of oranges. Gibraltar is like a white elephant in a zoological garden. It just eats and keeps off the flies with its short tail, and visitors feed it peanuts and wonder what it was made for, and how much hay it eats. Gibraltar is like a twenty-dollar gold piece that a man carries in his watch pocket for an emergency, which he never intends to spend until he gets in the tightest place of his life, and it wears out one pocket after another, and some day drops through on to the sidewalk, and a tramp finds it and goes on a bat and gets the worth of his money, and has a good time, if he saves enough to buy a bromo seltzer the next morning after. It is like the Russian war chest, that is never to be opened as long as they can borrow money. If Gibraltar could be put on castors, and rolled around from one country to another, England could whip all Europe and Asia. It would be a Tro Jane horse on a larger scale, and be a terror; but, say, if it got to America we wouldn't do a thing to it. We would run a standpipe up the side, and connect it with an oil pipe line, fill Gibraltar's tunnels and avenues, and magazines and barracks with crude oil, and touch a match to it, and not an Englishman would live to tell about it. Gee, but I would be sorry for the Irish soldiers, but I guess they wouldn't be there, cause they wouldn't fight America. Well, if England ever has a big war, and she gets chesty about Gibraltar, and says it is impregnable, and defies the world to take it, I bet you ten dollars it could be taken in twenty-four hours. If I was a general, or an admiral, I would have about forty tank steamers, loaded with kerosene, and have them land, innocent like, right up beside Gibraltar, ostensibly to sell oil for perfumery to the natives, who would all be improved by using kerosene on their persons. Then I would get on a barrel, on deck of my flag ship, and command the English general to surrender unconditionally, and if he refused I would set a slow match on every oil vessel, and have the crews get in skiffs and pull for the opposite shore, and when the oil got on fire, and rolled up all over Gibraltar, and burned every living thing, I would throw water from a fire department boat on the rock, and she would split open and roll all over-the prairie, and then I would bury the cremated dead out on the desert, and seek other worlds to conquer, like Alexander the Great. But don't be afraid. I won't do it unless they make me mad, but you watch my smoke if they pick on your little Hennery too much, when he grows up.

But I haven't got any kick coming about Gibraltar, cause they treated dad and I all right, and the commander detailed an ensign to show us all through the fortress. Now don't get an ensign mixed up with a unique, such as showed us through the Turkish harem. An English ensign is just as different from a Turkish unique as you can imagine. Every man to his place. You couldn't teach a Turkish unique how to show visitors around an English fortress, and an English ensign in a Turkish harem would bring on a world's war, they are so different. Well, we went through tunnels in the rock, and up and down elevators, and all was light as day from electric lights, and we saw ammunition enough to sink all the ships in the world, if it could be exploded in the right place, and they have provisions enough stored in the holes in the rock to keep an army for forty years if they didn't get ptomaine poisoned from eating canned stuff. It was all a revelation to dad, and when we got all through, and got out into the sunlight, we breathed free, and when dad got his second wind he broke up the English officers by taking out a pencil and piece of paper, and asked them what they would take for the rock and its contents, and move out, and let the American flag float over it. Well, say, they were hot, and they told dad to go plum to 'ell, but dad wouldn't do it. He said America didn't want the old stone quarry, anyway, and if it did it could come and take it. I guess they would have had dad arrested for treason, only when we got out into the town there was the whole British Atlantic squadron lined up, with the men up in the rigging like monkeys, and every vessel was firing a salute, as a yacht came steaming by. Dad thought war had surely broke out, or that some rich American owned the yacht, but it turned out to be Queen Alexandria and a party of tourists, and when the band played "God Save the Queen," dad got up on his hind legs and sang so loud you would think he would split hisself, and a fellow went up and threw his arms around dad, and began to weep, and the tears came in dad's eyes, and another fellow pinched dad's watch, and the celebration closed with everybody getting drunk, and the queen sailed away. Say, we are going to Spain, on the next boat, and you watch the papers. We will probably be hung for taking Cuba and the Phillipines.

  Yours,

  Hennery.

Sang So Loud You Would Think he Would Split Hisself 333

CHAPTER XXVII.

Madrid, Spain.—My Dear Uncle: You probably think we are taking our lives in our hands by coming to Spain, so soon after the Cuban war, in which President Roosevelt charged up San Juan Hill, in the face of over thirty bloodthirsty Spaniards, and captured the blockhouse on the summit of the hill, which was about as big as a switchman's shanty, and wouldn't hold two platoons of infantry, of twelve men to the platoon, without crowding, and which closed the war, after the navy had everlastingly paralyzed the Spanish vessels, and sunk them in wet water, and picked up the crews and run them through clothes-wringers to dry them out; but we are as safe here as we would be on South Clark street, in Chicago. Do you know, when I read of that charge of our troops up San Juan hill, headed by our peerless bear-hunter, I thought it was like the battle of Gettysburg, where hundreds of thousands of men fought on each side, and I classed Roosevelt with Grant, Sheridan, Sherman, Meade and Thomas, and all that crowd, but one day I got talking with a veteran of the Spanish-American war, who promptly deserted after every pay day, and re-enlisted after he had spent his money, and he didn't do a thing to my ideas of the importance of that battle. He told me it was only a little skirmish, like driving in a picket post, and that there were not Spaniards enough there to have a roll call, not so many Spanish soldiers as there were American newspaper correspondents on our side, that only a few were killed and wounded, and that a dozen soldiers in an army wagon could have driven up San Juan hill with firecrackers and scared the Spaniards out of the country, and that a part of a negro regiment did pretty near all the shooting, while our officers did the yelling, and had their pictures taken, caught in the act. So I have quit talking of the heroism of our army in Cuba, because it makes everybody laugh and they speak of Shaffer and Roosevelt, and hunch up their shoulders, and say, "bah," but when you talk about the navy, and Schley, and Sampson, and Clark, and Bob Evans, they take off their hats and their faces are full of admiration, and they say, "magnificent," and ask you to take a drink. Gee, but dad got his foot in it by talking about the blowing up of the Maine, and looking saucy, as though he was going to get even with the Spaniards, but he found that every Spaniard was as sorry for that accident as we were, and they would take off their hats when the Maine was mentioned, and look pained and heart-sick. I tell you the Spaniards are about as good people as you will find anywhere, and dad has concluded to fall back on Christopher Columbus for a steady diet of talk, cause if it had not been for Chris we wouldn't have been discovered to this day, which might have been a darn good thing for us. But the people here do not recall the fact that there ever was a man named Christopher Columbus, and they don't know what he ever discovered, or where the country is that he sailed away to find, unless they are educated, and familiar with ancient history, and only once in a while will you find anybody that is educated. The children of America know more about the history of Spain than the Spanish children. This country reminds you of a play on the stage, the grandees in their picturesque costumes, though few in number, compared to the population, are the whole thing, and the people you see on the stage with the grandees, in peasant costume, peddling oranges and figs, you find here in the life of Spain, looking up to the grandees as though they were gods. Every peasant carries a knife in some place, concealed about him, and no two carry their toad stabbers in the same place. If you see a man reach his finger under his collar to scratch his neck, the chances are his fingers touch the handle of his dagger, and if he hitches up his pants, his dagger is there, and if he pulls up his trousers leg to scratch for a flea, you can bet your life his knife is right handy, and if you have any trouble you don't know where the knife is coming from, as you do about an American revolver, when one of our citizens reaches for his pistol pocket. Spaniards are nervous people, on the move all the time, and it is on account of fleas. Every man, woman and child contains more than a million fleas, and as they can't scratch all the time, they keep on the move, hoping the fleas will jump off on somebody else. When we came here we were flealess, but every person we have come near to seems to have contributed some fleas to us, until now we are loaded down with them, and we find in our room at the hotel a box of insect powder, which, is charged in with the candles. The king, who is a boy about three years older than I am, is full of fleas, too, and he jumps around from one place to another, like he was shaking himself to get rid of them. He gets up in the morning and goes out horseback riding, and jumps fences and rides up and down the marble steps of the public buildings, as though he wanted to make the fleas feel in danger, so they will leave him. Seems to me if every man kept as many dogs as they do in Constantinople, the fleas would take to the dogs, but they say here that fleas will leave a dog to get on a human being, because they like the smell of garlic, as every Spaniard eats garlic a dozen times a day. They are trying to teach dogs to eat garlic, but no self-respecting dog will touch it. We have had to fill up on garlic in order to be able to talk with the people, cause dad got sea sick the first day here, everybody smelled so oniony. Dad wanted a druggist to put up onions in capsules, like they do quinine, so he could take onions and not taste them, but he couldn't make the man understand. There ought to be a law against any person eating onions, unless he is under a death sentence. But you can stand a man with the onion habit, after you get used to it. It is a woman, a beautiful woman, one you would like to have take you on your lap and pet you, that ought to know better than to eat onions. Gee, but when you see a woman that is so beautiful it makes her ache to carry her beauty around, and you get near to her and expect to breathe the odor of roses and violets, that makes you tired when she opens her mouth to say soft words of love, and there comes to your nostrils the odor of onions. Do you know, nothing would make me commit suicide so quick as to have a wife who habitually loaded herself with onions. Dad was buying some candy for me at a confectioner shop, of a beautiful Spanish woman, and when he asked how much it was, she bent over towards him in the most bewitching manner and breathed in his face and said, "Quatro-realis, seignor," which meant "four bits, mister," and he handed her a five-dollar gold piece, and went outdoors for a breath of fresh air, and let her keep the change. He said she was welcome to the four dollars and fifty cents if she would not breathe towards him again.

Breathed in his Face 339

Well, we have taken in the town, looked at the cathedrals, attended the sessions of the cortez, and thew gambling houses, saw the people sell the staple products of the country, which are prunes, tomatoes and wine. The people do not care what happens as long as they have a quart of wine. In some countries the question of existence is bread, but in Spain it is wine. No one is so poor they cannot have poor wine, and with wine nothing else is necessary, but a piece of cheese and bread helps the wine some, though either could be dispensed with. In some countries "wine, women and song" are all that is necessary to live. Here it is wine, cheese and an onion. We went to see the king, because he is such a young boy, and dad thought it would encourage the ruler to see an American statesman, and to mingle with an American boy who could give him cards and spades, and little casino, and beat him at any game. I made dad put on a lot of badges we had collected in our town when there were conventions held there, and when they were all pinned on dad's breast he looked like an admiral. There was a badge of Modern Woodmen, one of the Hardware Dealers' Association, one of the Wholesale Druggists, one of the Amalgamated Association of Railway Trainmen, one of the Farmers' Alliance, one of the Butter and Cheesemen's Convention, one of the State Undertakers' Guild, and half a dozen others in brass, bronze and tin, on various colored ribbons. Say, do you know, when they ushered us into the throne room at the palace, and the little king, who looked like a student in the high school, with dyspepsia from overstudy and cake between meals, saw dad, he thought he was the most distinguished American he had ever seen, and he invited dad up beside him on the throne, and dad sat in the chair that the queen will sit in when the boy king gets married, and I sat down on a front seat and watched dad. Dad had read in the papers that the boy king wanted to marry an American girl who was the possessor of a lot of money, so dad began to tell the king of girls in America that were more beautiful than any in the world, and had hundreds of millions of cold dollars, and an appetite for raw kings, and that he could arrange a match for the king that would make him richer than any king on any throne. The boy king was becoming interested, and I guess dad would have had him married off all right, if the king had not seen me take out a bag of candy and begin to eat, when he said to me, "Come up here, Bub, and give me some of that." Gosh, but I trembled like a leaf, but I went right up the steps of the throne and handed him the bag, and said, "Help yourself, Bub." Well, sir, the queerest thing happened. I had bought two pieces of candy filled with cayenne pepper, for April fool, and the king handed the bag to the master of ceremonies, a big Spaniard all covered over with gold lace, and if you will believe me the king got one piece of the cayenne pepper candy, and that spangled prime minister got the other, and the king chewed his piece first, and he opened his mouth like a dog that has picked up a hot boiled egg and he blew out his breath to cool his tongue and said, "Whoosh," and strangled, and sputtered, and then the prime minister he got his, and he yelled murder in Spanish, and the king called for water, and put his hands on his stomach and had a cramp, and the other man he tied himself up in a double bowknot, and called for a priest, and the king said he would have to go to the chapel, and the fellows who were guarding the king took him away, breathing hard, and red in the face, and dad said to me, "What the bloody hell you trying to do with the crowned heads? Cause you have poisoned the whole bunch, and we better get out."

So we went out of the palace while the king's retainers were filling him with ice water. Well, they got the cayenne pepper out of him, because we saw him at the bull fight in the afternoon, but for a while he had the hottest box there ever was outside of a freight train, and if he lives to be as old as Mr. Methuselah he will always remember his interview with little Hennery. The bull fights ain't much. Bulls come in the ring mad as wet hens, cause they stick daggers in them, and they bellow around, and the Spaniards dodge and shake red rags at them, and after a bull has ripped a mess of bowels out of a few horses, then a man with a saber stabs the bull between the shoulders, and he drops dead, and the crowd cheers the assassin of the bull, and they bring in another bull. Well, sir, dad came mighty near his finish at the bull fight. When the second bull came in, and ripped the stomach out of a blind horse, and the bull was just charging the man who was to stab it, dad couldn't stand it any longer and he climbed right over into the ring, and he said: "Look a here, you heathen; I protest, in the name of the American Humane Society, against this cruelty to animals, and unless this business stops right here I will have this place pulled, and———"

Dad Couldn't Stand It Any Longer 343

Well, sir, you would of thought that bull would have had sense enough to see that dad was his friend, but he probably couldn't understand what dad was driving at, for he made a rush for dad, and dad started to run for the fence, and the bull caught dad just like dad was sitting in a rocking chair, and tossed him over the fence, and dad's pants stayed on the bull's horns, and dad landed in amongst a lot of male and female grandees and everybody yelled, "Bravo, Americano," and the police wrapped a blanket around dad's legs and were going to take him to the emergency hospital, but I claimed dad, and took him to the hotel. Dad is ready to come home now. He says he is through.

Yours,
Hennery.

Dad's Pants Stayed on the Bull's Horns 349

CHAPTER XXVIII.

Berlin, Germany.—My Dear Old Pummer-nickel: Now we have got pretty near home, and you would enjoy it to be with us, because you couldn't tell the town from Milwaukee, except for the military precision with which everything is conducted, where you never take a glass of beer without cracking your heels together like a soldier, and giving a military salute to the bartender, who is the commander-in-chief of all who happen to patronize his bar. Everybody here acts like he was at a picnic in the woods, with a large barrel of beer, with perspiration oozing down the outside, and a spigot of the largest size, which fills a schooner at one turn of the wrist, and every man either smiles or laughs out loud, and you feel as though there was happiness everywhere, and that heaven was right here in this greatest German city.

There is Laughter Everywhere 353

There is laughter everywhere, except when the Emperor drives by, escorted by his bodyguard, on the finest horses in the world; then every citizen on the street stops smiling and laughing; all stand at attention, and every face takes on a solemn, patriotic, almost a fighting look, as though each man would consider it his happiest duty and pleasure to walk right up to the mouth of cannon and die in his tracks for his pale-faced, haggard and loved Emperor. And the Emperor never smiles on his subjects as he passes, but looks into every eye on both sides of the beautiful street, with an expression of agony on his face, but a proud light in his eye, as though he would say, "Ach, Gott, but they are daisies, and they would fight for the Fatherland with the last breath in their bodies."

The pride of the people in that moustached young man, with the look of suffering, is only equalled by the pride of the Emperor in every German in Germany, or anywhere on the face of the globe. There is none of the "Hello, Bill!" such as we have in America, when the President drives through his people, many of whom yell, "Hello, Teddy!" while he shows his teeth, and laughs, and stands up in his carriage, and says, "Hello, Mike," as he recognizes an acquaintance. But these same "Hello, Bill," Americans are probably just as loyal to their chief, whoever he may be, and would fight as hard as the loving Germans would for their hereditary Emperor.

I suppose there is somebody working in Berlin, but it seems to us that the whole population, so far as can be seen, is bent on enjoying every minute, walking the streets, in good clothes, giving military salutes, and drinking beer between meals, and talking about what Germany would do to an enemy if the ever-present chip on the shoulder should be knocked off, even accidentally. But they all seem to love America, and when we registered at the hotel, from Milwaukee, Wis., U. S. A., citizens began to gather around us and ask about relatives at our home. They seem to think that every German who has settled in Milwaukee owns a brewery, and that all are rich, and that some day they will come back to Germany and spend the money, and fight for the Emperor.

We did not have the heart to tell them that all the Germans in Milwaukee were going to stay there and spend their money, and while their hearts were still warm towards the Fatherland, they loved the Stars and Stripes, and would fight for the American flag, against the world, and that the younger Germans spoke the German language, if it all, with a Yankee accent. Gee, but wouldn't the people of Berlin be hot under the collar if they knew how many Germans in America were unfamiliar with the make-up of the German flag, and that they only see it occasionally when some celebration of German days takes place.

Well, when dad saw the German Emperor drive down the great street, and got a look at his face, he said, "Hennery, I have got to see that young man and advise him to go and consult a doctor," and so we made arrangements to go to the Palace and see the Emperor and his son, the Crown Prince, who will before long take the empire on his shoulders, if William is as sick as he looks. You don't have to hire any masquerade clothes to call on the Emperor of Germany, like you do when you visit royalty in Turkey and Egypt, for a good frock coat and a silk hat will take you anywhere in the day time, and a swallowtail is legal tender at night; so dad put on his frock coat and silk hat, just as he would to go and attend an afternoon wedding at home, and we were ushered in to a regular parlor, where the Emperor was having fun with his children, and the Empress was doing some needlework.

Dad supposed we would have to talk to the Emperor and the Prince through an interpreter, and we stood there waiting for some one to break the ice, when some one told the Emperor that an American gentleman and his boy wanted to pay their respects, and the Emperor, who wore an ordinary dark suit, with no military frills, took one of the young Princes he had been playing with across his knee and gave him a couple of easy spanks, in fun, and the whole family was laughing, and the spanked boy "tackled" the Emperor around the legs, below the knee, like a football player, and the other Princes pulled him off, and the Emperor came up to dad, smiling as though he was having the time of his life, and spoke to dad in the purest English, and said he was glad to see the "Bad Boy" man, because he had read all about the pranks of the Bad Boy, and bid dad welcome to Germany, and he didn't look sick at all.

And So This is the Champion Little Devil of America 357

Dad was taken all of a heap, and didn't know what to make of the German Emperor talking English, but when the ruler of Germany turned to me and said, "And so this is the champion little devil of America," and patted me on the head, dad felt that he had struck a friend of the family, and he sat down with the Emperor and talked for half an hour, while the young Princes gathered around me, and we sat down on the floor and the boys got out their knives, and we played mumbletypeg on the carpet, just as though we were at home, and all the boys talked English, and we had a bully time. The princes had all read "Peck's Bad Boy" and I think the Emperor and Empress have encouraged them in their wickedness, for the boys told me of several tricks they had played on their father, the Emperor, which they had copied from the Bad Boy, and it made me blush when they told of initiating their father into the Masons, the way my chum and I initiated dad into the Masons with the aid of a goat.

I asked the boys how their dad took it, and told them from what we in America heard about the Emperor of Germany, we would think he would kill anybody that played a trick on him; but they said he would stand anything from the children, and enjoy it; but if grown men attempted to monkey with him, the fur would fly. The Crown Prince came in and was introduced to me, and he seemed proud to see me, cause his uncle, Prince Henry, had told him about being in

Milwaukee, and how all the women in that town were the handsomest he had ever seen in his trip around the world, and he asked me if it was so. I referred him to dad, and dad told him the women were the greatest in the world, and then dad made his usual break. He said: "Look ahere, Mister Prince, you have got to be married some day, and raise a family to hand the German empire down to, and my advice to you is not to let them saw off on to you no duchess or princess as homely as a hedge fence, with no ginger in her blood, but you skip out to America, and come to Milwaukee, and I will introduce you to girls that are so handsome they will make you toe the mark, and if you marry one of them she will raise a family of healthy young royalty with no humor in the blood, and you won't have to go off and be gay away from home, cause an American wife will take you by the ear if you show any signs of wandering from your own fireside, like lots of your relatives have done."

Gee, but that made the Emperor hot, and he said dad needn't instill any of his American ideas into the German nobility, as he could run things all right without any help, and dad got ready to go, cause the atmosphere was getting sort of chilly, but the Emperor soon got over his huff, and told dad not to hurry, and then he turned to me and said, "Now, little American Bad Boy, what kind of a trick are you going to play on me, 'cause from what I have read of you I know you will never go out of this house without giving me a benefit, and all my boys expect it, and will enjoy it, the same as I will; now, let 'er go."

I felt that it was up to me to do something to maintain the reputation I had made, so I said, "Your majesty, I will now proceed to make it interesting for you, if you and the boys will kindly be seated in a circle around me." They got into a circle, all laughing, and I took out of my pistol pocket a half pint flask, of glass, covered with leather, and with a stopper that opened by touching a spring, and I walked around in front of each one of the Royal family, mumbling, "Ene-mene-mony-my," and opening the flask in front of each one, and pretty soon they all began to get nervous, and scratch themselves, and the Emperor slapped his leg, and pinched his arm, and put his fingers down his collar and scratched his neck, and the Crown Prince jumped up and kicked his leg, and scratched his back, and said, "Say, kid, you are not hypnotizing us, are you?" and I said, "Ene-meny-mony-my," and kept on touching the stopper.

By and by they all got to scratching, and the Emperor turned sort of pale, but he was going to see the show through to the end, as long as he had a ticket, and he said, "What is the joke, anyway?" and I kept on saying, "Ene-mene-mony-my," and walking around in front of them, and dad began to dance around, too, and dig under his shirt bosom, and scratch his leg, and then they all scratched in unison, and laughed, and a little prince asked how long before they would know what it was all about, and I said my ene-mene, and looked solemn, and dad said, "What you giving us?" and I said, "Never you mind; this is my show, and I am the whole push," and everybody had raised up out of his chair and each was scratching for all that was out, and finally the Emperor said, "I like a joke as well as anybody, but I can't laugh until I know what I am laughing about," and he told dad to make me show what was in the bottle, and I showed the bottle and there was nothing in it, and there they stood scratching themselves, and I told dad we better excuse ourselves and go, and we were going all right enough when dad said, "What is it you are doing?" and as we got almost to the door I said, "Your majesty, I have distributed, impartially, I trust, in the Royal family of Germany, a half a pint of the hungriest fleas that Egypt can produce, for they have been in that flask three weeks, with nothing to eat except themselves, and I estimate that there were a million Cairo fleas in the flask, enough to set up housekeeping in your palace, with enough to stock the palace of your Crown Prince when he is married, and this is that you may remember the visit of Peck's Bad Boy and his Dad."

Dad Leaned Against a Lamp Post and Scratched his Back 364

The Emperor was mad at first, but he laughed, and when we got out of the palace dad leaned against a lamp post and scratched his back, and said to me, "Hennery, you never ought to have did it," and I said, "What could a poor boy do when called upon suddenly to do something to entertain royalty?"

"Well," says dad, "I don't care for myself, but this thing is apt to bring on international complications," and I said, "Yes, it will bring Persia into it, cause they will have to use Persian insect powder to get rid of them," and then we went to our hotel and fought fleas all night, and thought of the sleepless night the royal family were having.

Well, so long, old Pummernickel.

Your only,

Hennery.

CHAPTER XXIX.

Brussels, Belgium.—Dear Old Skate: "What is the matter with our going to Belgium?" said dad to me, as we were escaping from Germany. "Well, what in thunder do we want to go to Belgium for?" said I to dad. "I do not want to go to a country that has no visible means of support, except raising Belgian hares, to sell to cranks in America. I couldn't eat rabbits without thinking I was chewing a piece of house cat, and rabbits is the chief food of the people. I have eaten horse and mule in Paris, and wormy figs in Turkey, and embalmed beef fried in candle grease in Russia, and sausage in Germany, imported from the Leutgart sausage factory in Chicago, where the man run his wife through a sausage machine; and stuff in Egypt, with ground mummy for curry powder, but I draw the line on Belgian hares, and I strike right here, and shall have the International Union of Amalgamated Tourists declare a boycott on Belgium, by gosh," said I, just like that, bristling up to dad real spunky.

"You are going to Belgium all right," said dad, as he took hold of my thumb in a Jiu Jitsu fashion, and twisted it backwards until I fairly penuked, and held it, while he said he should never dare go home without visiting King Leopold's kingdom, and had a talk with an eighty-year-old male flirt, who had a thousand chorus girls on his staff, and could give the Sultan of Turkey cards and spades and little casino in the harem game. "You will go along, won't you, bub?" and he gave my thumb another twist, and I said, "You bet your life, but I won't do a thing to you and Leopold before we get out of the Belgian hare belt," and so here we are, looking for trouble.

It is strange we never hear more about Belgium in America, but actually I never heard of a Belgian settling in the United States. There are Irish, and Germans, and Norwegians, and Italians, and men of all other countries, but I never saw a Belgian until to-day, and it does you good to see a people who don't do anything but work. There is not a loafer in Belgium, and every man has smut on his nose, and his hands are black with handling iron, or something. There is no law against people going away from Belgium, but they all like it here, and seem to think there is no other country, and they are happy, and work from choice.

"Began to sell dad relics of the Battle of Waterloo."

I always knew the Belgian guns that sell in America for twelve shillings, and kill at both ends, but I never knew they made things here that were worth anything, but dad says they are better fixed here for making everything used by civilized people than any country on earth, and I am glad to be here, cause you get notice when you are going to be robbed. They ring a bell here every minute to give you notice that some one is after the coin, so when you hear a bell ring, if you hang onto your pocketbook, you don't lose.

This is the place where "There was a sound of revelry at night, and Belgium's capitol had gathered there." You remember, the night before the Battle of Waterloo, when Napoleon Bonaparte got his. You must remember about it, old man, just when they were right in the midst of the dance, and "soft eyes looked love to eyes which spake again," and they were taking a champagne bath, inside and out, when suddenly the opening guns of Waterloo, twelve miles away, began to boom, and the poet, who was present, said, "But hush, hark, a deep sound like a rising knell," and everybody turned pale and began to stampede, when the floor manager said, "'Tis but the wind, or the car on the stony street, on with the dance, let joy be unconfined, no sleep till morn, when youth and pleasure meet, to chase the glowing hours with flying feet."

Well, sir, this is the place where that ball took place, which is described in the piece I used to speak in school, but I never thought I would be here, right where the dancers got it in the neck. When dad found that the battlefield of Waterloo was only a few miles away, he hired a wagon and we went out there. Well, sir, of all the frauds we have run across on this trip the battlefield of Waterloo is the worst. When the farmers who are raising barley and baled hay on the battlefield, saw us coming, they dropped their work and made a rush for us, and one fellow yelled something in the Belgian language that sounded like, "I saw them first," and he got hold of dad and me, and the rest stood off like a lot of hack drivers that have seen a customer fall into the hands of another driver, and made up faces at us, and called the farmer who had caught us the vilest names. They said we would be skinned to a finish by the faker who got us, and they were right.

368 Began to Sell Things To Dad

He showed us from a high hill, where the different portions of the battle were fought, and where they caught Napoleon Bonaparte, and where Blucher came up and made things hum in the German language, and then he took us off to his farm where the most of the relics were found, and began to sell things to dad, until he had filled the hind end of the wagon with bullets and grape-shot, sabres and bayonets, old rusty rifles, and everything dad wanted, and we had enough to fill a museum, and when the farmer had got dad's money we went back to Brussels, and got our stuff unloaded at the hotel. Say, when we came to look it over we found two rusty Colt's revolvers, and guns of modern construction, which have been bought on battlefields in all countries, and properly rusted to sell to tourists. I showed dad that the revolver was unknown at the time of the battle of Waterloo, and that every article he had bought was a fraud, the sabers having been made in America, before the war of the rebellion, and dad was mad, and gave the stuff to the porter of the hotel, who charged dad seven dollars for taking it away.

Dad kept one three-cornered hat that the farmer told him Bonaparte lost when his horse stampeded with him, and it drifted under a barbed wire fence, where it had lain until the day before we visited the battlefield. Say, that hat is as good as new, and dad says it is worth all the stuff cost, but I would not be found dead wearing it, cause it is all out of style.

We have seen the King of Belgium, and actually got the worth of our money. He is an old dandy, and looks like a Philadelphia Quaker, only he is not as pious as a Quaker. Dad wrote to the King and said he was a distinguished American, traveling for his health, and had a niece who had frequently visited Belgium with an opera company, and she had spoken of the King, and dad wanted to talk over matters that might be of interest both to Belgium and to America. Well, the messenger came back and said dad couldn't get to the palace a minute too quick, and so we went over, and as we were going through the park we saw an old man, in citizen's clothes, sitting on a bench, patting the head of a boar hound, and when he saw us he said, "Come here, Uncle Sam, and let my dog chew your pants." Dad thought it must be some lunatic, and was going to make a sneak, and get out, when the man rose up and we saw it was the King, and we went up to him and sat down on the bench, and he asked dad if he had come as the relative of the opera singer, to commence suit against the King for breach of promise, or to settle for a money consideration, remarking that he had always rather pay cash than to have any fuss made about these little matters. Dad told him he had no claim against him for alienating anybody's affections, or for breach of promise, and that all he wanted was to have a little talk with the King, and find out how a King lived, and how he had any fun in running the king business, at his age, and they sat down and began to talk as friendly as two old chums, while the dog played tag with me. We found that the King was a regular boy, and that instead of his mind being occupied by affairs of state, or his African concessions in the Congo country, where he owns a few million slaves who steal ivory for him, and murder other tribes, he was enjoying life just as he did when he was a barefooted boy, fishing for perch at the old mill pond, and when he mentioned his career as a boy, and his enjoyments, dad told about his youth, and how he never got so much pleasure in after life as he did when he had a stone bruise on his heel, and went off into the woods and cut a tamarack pole and caught sunfish till the cows came home.

The King brightened up and told dad he had a pond in the palace grounds, stocked with old-fashioned fish, and every day he took off his shoes and rolled up his pants, and with nothing on but a shirt and pants held up by one suspender of striped bed ticking, he went out in a boat and fished as he did when a boy, with a bent pin for a hook, and he was never so happy as when so engaged, and they could all have their grand functions, and balls, and dinners, and Turkish baths, if they wanted them, but give him the old swimming hole. "Me, too," said dad, and as dad looked down into the park he saw a little lake, and dad held up two fingers, just as boys do when they mean to say, "Come on, let's go in swimming," and the King said, "I'll go you," and they locked arms and started through the woods to the little lake, and the dog and I followed.

Dad and Leopold Make a Rush for That Swimming Place 372

Well, sir, you'd a dide to see dad and Leopold make a rush for that swimming place. The King put his hand in the water, and said it was fine, and began to peel his clothes off, and dad took off his clothes and the King made a jump and went in all over, and came up with his eyes full of water, strangling because he did not hold his nose, and then dad made a leap and splashed the water like an elephant had fallen in, and there those two old men were in the lake, just like kids.

I'll Swim You a Match to the Other Side 378

"I'll swim you a match to the other side," said the King. "It's a go," said dad, and they started porpoising across the little lake, and then I thought it was time there was something doing; so I got busy and tied their clothes in knots so tight you couldn't get them untied without an act of parliament. They went ashore on the opposite side of the lake, cause some women were driving through the grounds, and then I found a flock of goats grazing on the lawn, and the dog and I drove them to where the clothes were tied in knots, and when the goats began to chew the clothes I took the dog and went back to the entrance of the park, and dad and the King swam back to where the clothes and the goats were, and when they drove the goats away, and couldn't untie the knots, the King gave the grand hailing sign of distress, or something, and the guards of the palace and some cavalry came on the run, and the park seemed filled with an army, and I bid the dog good-bye, and went back to the hotel alone and waited for dad.

When the Goats Began to Chew The Clothes

Dad didn't get back till after dark, and when he came he had on a suit of the King's clothes, too tight around the stomach, and too long in the legs, cause dad is pusey, and the King is long-geared. "Did you have a good time, dad?" says I, and he said, "Haven't you got any respect for age, condemn you? The King has ordered that you be fed to the animals in the zoo." I told him I didn't care a darn what they did with me; I had been brought up to tie knots in clothes when I saw people in swimming, and I didn't care whether they were crowned heads or just plain dubs, and I asked dad how they got along when their clothes were chewed up. He said the soldiers covered them with pouches and got them to the palace, and they had supper, he and the King, and the servants brought out a lot of clothes and he got the best fit he could. I asked him if the King was actually mad, and he said no, that he always enjoyed such things, and wanted dad and I to come the next day and go fishing with him, barefooted. Say, dad can go, but I wouldn't be caught by that King on a bet. He would get even, sure, cause he has a look in his eye like they have in a sanitarium. Not any king business for your little Hennery.

CHAPTER XXX.

Havana, Cuba. My Dear Old Greaser: We stopped in Holland for a couple of days after we left Belgium, and it was the most disappointing country we visited on our whole trip. We expected to be walked on with wooden shoes, and from what we had heard of that Duke that married Queen Wilhelmina, we thought we were going to a country where men were cruel to their wives, and swatted them over the head when things didn't go right, but when we saw the queen riding with her husband, as free, from ostentation as a department store clerk would ride out with his cash girl wife, and saw happiness beaming on the face of the queen and her husband, and saw them squeeze hands and look lovingly into each other's eyes, we made up our minds that you couldn't believe these newspaper scandals. And when we saw the broad-shouldered, broad-chested and broad-everywhere women of Holland we concluded that it would be a brave or reckless husband who would be unkind to one of them, and mighty dangerous because the women are stronger than the men, and any woman could whip four men at the drop of the hat, because she could take off her wooden shoes and strike out and a man would think he had been hit by a railroad tie.

Illustration: Any woman could whip four men at the drop of the hat 388

I do not know what makes Hollanders wear wooden shoes, unless they are sentenced to do it, or that they are unruly, and have to be hobbled, to keep them from jumping fences, but the people are so good and honest that after you have met them you forget the vaudeville feature of their costumes, and love them, and wish the people of other countries were as honest as they. For two or three days we were not robbed, and I do not believe there is a dishonest man or woman in Holland, except one. There was one woman that played it on dad in Amsterdam, but I think she only played him for a sucker for a joke, for she laughed all the time.

Dad was much struck at seeing the women selling milk from little carts, hauled by teams of big dogs, and he negotiated with a woman for a dog team and cart, and all one day dad and I put on wooden shoes, and Dutch clothes and drove the dog team around town, and we had the time of our lives, more fun than I ever had outside of a circus, but the shoes skinned our feet, and when the dogs laid down to rest, and dad couldn't talk dog language to make them get up and go ahead, he kicked the off dog with his wooden shoe, and the dog got up and grabbed a mouthful of dad's ample pants and shook dad till his teeth were loose.

Grabbed a Mouthful of Dad's Ample Pants 386

A woman driving another mess of dogs had to come and choke the off dog so he wouldn't swallow dad, pants and all. Dad gave her a dollar for rescuing him, and what do you think? Say, she pulled an old stocking of money out of her bosom and counted out ninety-six cents in change and gave it back to dad, and only charged four cents for saving his life, and that couldn't occur in any other country, cause in most places they would take the dollar and strike him for more.

Dad wanted to take the dog team and cart to Milwaukee to give it to a friend who sells red hot weiners, and so we arranged to have the team loaded on the boat, but just before the boat sailed, the dog team was lying down on the dock, sleeping and scratching flees, when the woman dad bought the team of came along and spoke to the dogs in Dutch, and, say, those dogs woke up and started on a regular runaway down the dock, after the laughing woman, and disappeared up the street. Just as the boat whistled to pull in the gang planks, dad and I stood on deck and saw the team disappear, and dad said, "Buncoed again, by gosh, and it is all your condemned fault. Why didn't you hang on to that off dog." Well, we lost our dog team, but we got the worth of our money, for we saw a people who do not eat much beside cabbage and milk, and they are the strongest in the world, and there never was a case of dyspepsia in their country. We saw a people with stone bruises on their heels and corns on their toes, smiling and laughing all the time. We met a people that work all the time, and never take any recreation except churning and rocking babies, and yet never have to call a doctor, because there are no doctors except veterinary surgeons, who care for dogs and cattle.

The people we met in Holland wear wooden shoes to teach them patience and humility. With wooden shoes no frenzied financier of Holland will ever travel the fast road of speculation, slip on a bucket-shop banana peel, and fall on the innocent bystander who has coughed up his savings and given them to the honest financier to safely invest.

The bank of Holland is an old woolen stock ing, and money never comes out of the stocking unless there is a string to it, and the string is the heart string of an honest people, that will stand no trifling. If a dishonest financier came to Holland from any other country, and did any of his dirty work, the women of Holland, who handle the funds, would give him such a hazing that he would never open his three-card monte lay-out in any other country.

It is a country where you get the right change back, and the cows give eighteen carat milk, and the hens have not learned to lay small, cold storage eggs. It is the country for me, if the women would wear corsets, and not be the same size all the way down, so that if you hugged a girl you wouldn't make a dent in her, that would not come out until she got her breath.

And we left such a country and such a people, to come here to Cuba, where the population now comprises the meanest features of the desperate and wicked Spaniards, beaten at their own game of loot, the trickiness of the native Cuban, flushed with pride because his big American brother helped him to drive away the Spaniard that he could never have gotten rid of alone, and with no respect for the American who helped, and only meets him respectfully because he is afraid of being thrown into the ocean if he is impudent, and the worst class of Yankee grafters and highway robbers that have ever been allowed to stray away from the land of the free. That is what Cuba is to-day.

Soulless Yankee corporations have got hold of most of the branches of business that there is any money in, and the things that do not pay and never can be made to pay, are for sale to tenderfeet. The cuban hates the Yankee, the Yankee hates the Cuban, and the Spaniard hates both, and both hate him. In Havana your hotel, owned by a Cuban, run by a Yankee, with a Spanish or Portuguese cashier, will take all the money you bring into it for a bed at night, and hold your baggage till your can cable for money to buy breakfast. It is a "free country," of course, run by men who will fly high as long as they can borrow money for some one else to pay after they are dead, but within ten years the taxes will eat the people so they will be head over heels in debt to the Yankee and the Spaniard, the German and the Englishman, the Frenchman and the Italian, and some day warships will sail into Havana harbor, over the submerged bones of the "Maine," and there will be a fight for juicy morsels of the Cuban dead horse, by the congregated buzzards of strange navies, unless they shall shake the dice for the carcass, and by carefully loading the dice saw the whole thing off on to Uncle Sam, and make him pay the debts of the deceased republic, and act as administrator for the benefit of the children of the sawed off republic, whose only asset now is climate that feels good, but contains germs of all diseases, and tobacco that smells good when it is in conflagration under your nose, and does not kill instantly if it is pasted up in a Wisconsin wrapper, that is the pure goods. If tobacco ever ceases to be a fad with the rich consumer of fifty-cent cigars, and beet sugar is found to contain no first aid to Bright's disease, Cuba will amount to about as much as Dry Tortugas, which has purer air, and the Isle of Pines, which has more tropical scenery and less yellow fever. But now the Island of Cuba is a joy, and Havana is like Heaven, until you come to pay your bill, when it is hell. Streets so wide you cannot see a creditor on the other side, pavements as smooth as the road to perdition, and tropical trees, plants and flowers, with birds of rare plumage, you feel like sitting on a cold bench in the shade, and wishing all your friends were here to enjoy a taste of what will come to those who are truly good, in the hereafter, when suddenly you are taken with a chill up the spinal column, and a cold sweat comes out on the forehead, and the internal arrangements go on a strike because of the cold, perspiring cucumber you had for lunch, and you go to the doctor, who does not do a thing to you, but scare you out of your boots by talking of cholera, and giving you the card of his partner, the undertaker, telling you never to think of dying in a tropical country without being embalmed, because you look so much better when you are delivered at your home by the express company, and then he gives you pills and a bill, and an alarm clock that goes off every hour to take a pill by, and furnishes you an officer to go home to your hotel with you to collect his bill, and you pawn your watch and sleeve buttons for a steerage ticket to New York, where you arrive as soon as the Lord will let you, and stay as long as He thinks is good for you.

Dad has not been much good in Havana, cause he wanted to see the whole business in one day. He got a row boat and went out in the harbor to where the back-bone of the "Maine" acts as a monument to the fellows who yet sleep in the mud of the bottom, and after tying a little American flag on the rigging that sticks up above the water, and damning the villains who blew up the good ship, we went back to town and drove out to the cemetery where several hundred of our boys are buried, where we left flowers on the graves and a cuss in the balmy air for the guilty wretches who fired the bomb, and then we went back to the city and walked the beautiful streets, until dad began to have cramps, from trying to eat all the fruit he could hold, and then it was all off, and I was going to call a carriage to take him to the hotel, when dad saw a negro astride a single ox, hitched to a cart, who had come in from the country, and dad said he wanted to ride in that cart, if it was the last act of his life, and as dad was beginning to swell up from the fruit he had eaten, I thought he better ride in an open cart, cause in a carriage he might swell up so we couldn't get him out of the door when we got to the hotel, so I hired the negro, got dad in the cart, and we started, but the ox walked so slow I was afraid we would never get dad there alive, so I told the negro dad had the cholera, and that settled, for he kicked the slats of the ox in with his heels, and the ox bellowed and run away, and the negro turned pale from fright, and I guess the runaway ride on the cobble stone pavement was what saved dad's life, for the swelling in dad's inside began to go down, and when we got to the hotel he got out of the cart alone, and I knew he was better, for he shook himself, gulluped up wind, and said, "You think you are smart, don't you?" So I will close.

 Yours,
 Hennery.

Made in the USA
Lexington, KY
12 July 2016